READY TO
WIN OVER
DEPRESSION

THELMA
WELLS

HARVEST HOUSE PUBLISHERS

EUGENE, OREGON

Published in association with Van Diest Literary Agency, PO Box 1482, Sisters, Oregon 97759, www.lastchapterpublishing.com

Cover by Koechel Peterson & Associates, Inc., Minneapolis, Minnesota

Cover photo © Stockxpert / Jupiter Images Unlimited

READY TO WIN OVER DEPRESSION
Copyright © 2010 by Thelma Wells
Published by Harvest House Publishers
Eugene, Oregon 97402
www.harvesthousepublishers.com

Library of Congress Cataloging-in-Publication Data
    Wells, Thelma.
    Ready to win over depression / Thelma Wells.
        p. cm.
    ISBN 978-0-7369-2824-3 (pbk.)
    1. Depression, Mental—Religious aspects—Christianity. 2. Depressed persons—Religious life. I. Title.
    BV4910.34.W45 2010
    248.8'625–dc22

                                                    2009038628

Printed in the United States of America

        10 11 12 13 14 15 16 17 18 / VP-SK / 10 9 8 7 6 5 4 3 2 1

*To those of you who feel
paralyzed by feelings of depression.
I'm asking God to make His presence known to you.
He will help you persevere through the pain and sorrow until
you experience the full and marvelous light of
hope and peace found in Christ Jesus.*

*I also dedicate this book to those of you who have
made it through depression and are reaching out to others
still in distress. Thank you for caring.
I'm praying that God will bless you and
the people you're helping.*

Depression + Hope in God = Freedom!

*Friends, you all deserve to be free and to live a life of joy
and laughter. Let me help you find your way.
You can "experience God's peace, which exceeds
anything we can understand. His peace will
guard your hearts and minds as you live in Christ Jesus"*
(NEW LIVING TRANSLATION).

Acknowledgment

A special thank you to comedian and recording artist Chonda Pierce. Chonda, your humility and willingness to write the Foreword for this book is much appreciated. Thank you for sharing your heart so readers will know that with God they *can* kick depression out of their lives and enjoy the sweet peace and joy of Jesus. With Christ, each day is sweeter than the last.

Contents

∞

Foreword

I was diagnosed with clinical depression several years ago. As a comedian, I was convinced that I'd never laugh again. As a Christian, I was convinced that others would see this as a flaw in my ministry. Both of those thoughts were part of the lies that depression whispers in your ear.

Thelma has written an honest book that is not only inspiring but has become another tool I have in my own little doctor's kit from the Great Physician.

Chonda Pierce

Our Journey Together

Yes, I've been there. I was in depression for a couple of years. I know what it's like. And I'm often reminded that *so many of us* have been there as well—or are there at this very moment. I'm told, in fact, that more people suffer from depression today than any other physical or mental affliction. Isn't that something? The number of afflicted is in the millions, and my heart goes out to them…and to you, for no doubt you've picked up this book because either you or someone very close to you is battling depression right now.

You and I are going to face that struggle together in this book. But before we look directly at the topic of depression, I want to start by projecting a picture in your mind of someone I identify with so strongly—and yet I don't even know her name. At the time, she was just another face in the crowd…and I suspect that's the way she wanted it.

Down Low

This woman wasn't well. Physically she didn't feel good at all. It's likely that she was also depressed, though I'm not absolutely certain about that. What I know for sure is that she had health problems—*female* problems—for 12 years. As someone who's suffered my own female problems, I can understand why she probably preferred to remain anonymous. Can you spell *h-o-r-m-o-n-a-l?*

She'd been to many doctors, but none had been able to stop her flow of blood. Surely any woman of any era could understand how frustrated and miserable she must have felt. Enduring such problems in today's "disposable everything," wash-and-wear world is hassle enough. But imagine having such a problem for that many years when nothing was reusable and laundry was scrubbed by hand on the riverbank. In the time this woman lived, the embarrassment of her condition was exacerbated by the law of the day that said a woman bleeding was "ceremonially unclean" (Leviticus 15:19-25). Drawing from Leviticus 13:45, she might have been required to announce loudly "Unclean, unclean!" as she moved through a crowd so people could avoid her and not get defiled by touching her.

You see, this woman I'm speaking of is introduced to us in the Bible. There are other folks in Scripture who clearly suffered from depression (we'll look at some of them later), and while this woman might or might not be one of them, she nevertheless offers a fascinating profile as we consider how to overcome this malady.

This lady was in a crowd surrounding Jesus one day as He made His way through the streets. Perhaps she wasn't bold enough to push her way to the front of the throng to catch His eye. Matthew, Mark, and Luke all say, as they tell her story in their Gospels, that she "came up behind him."

Despite her weakness and timidity, on that day she had such unshakable faith that she thought, "If I touch even his garments, I will be made well" (Mark 5:28). And that's what she did. Matthew's account says she touched "the fringe of his garment."

Only the *fringe*? Just the *hem*? My mind tries to picture how *that* could have been the part of Jesus' clothing she managed to touch amid the surging crowd. How did she get so low? Perhaps she was knocked down by the press of the multitude—and *still* she didn't give up. Her faith and determination were that strong.

And Jesus knew it. As soon as her fingertips brushed over the fibers in the hem of His cloak, He "immediately turned about in the crowd and said, 'Who touched my garments?'" (Mark 5:30).

Now that's a rather strange question (and His disciples thought so too). Here's this mass of people pressing around Jesus, yet He suddenly stops and asks who touched Him. Wasn't He being touched by practically everybody there?

But Jesus wasn't kidding. He'd felt power go out of Him when the woman made her move, and now He was looking through the sea of faces to find her. Then the woman, "knowing what had happened to her, came in fear and trembling and fell down before him and told him the whole truth" (verse 33).

Of course she wasn't telling Jesus anything He didn't already know. In fact, at that point they *both* knew what had happened. Jesus spoke to her to let the crowd in on the secret: "Daughter, your faith has made you well; go in peace, and be healed of your disease" (verse 34).

Oh, to have the determined, undistracted faith of this anonymous woman! Until Jesus spoke to her, she was a silent nobody in the crowd that day. But 2000 years later the story of what she experienced still speaks to us in an unforgettable way. She knew Jesus had the power to change her life for good.

And I, for one, know He still has that power today.

All Planned Out

Like I said, I know about "female problems." Just a few years ago I was one of the speakers on the Women of Faith tour. We were headed into the busiest part of the season, and I was getting very, very tired. We were traveling so much, and I had so much going on, I thought getting tired was perfectly normal. There were other symptoms ("female" things), but not enough to alarm me—at least at first. But eventually the problems bothered me so much I went to the doctor for some tests. When the reports came back he recommended a hysterectomy.

I talked to several women who'd had hysterectomies, and they said, "Oh, girl! That's gonna be the best thing for you. You'll be so happy! You'll feel great after it's over."

Let me just say, if you're one of those women who told me those things, don't you be talking sweet to me now, okay? No, ma'am! If you do, I may give in to an overwhelming urge to hit you upside the head. Well, no, I wouldn't resort to violence, but I would have some thoughts to share with you.

I agreed to have the surgery, and I laid out the schedule the doctor and I would follow. My last speaking engagement of the year was December 7. I would have the surgery December 8, and come home by December 11. A week later I would trot into the doctor's office for the follow-up exam. By Christmas I would preside as usual over my family's annual holiday celebration. A couple of weeks later I'd be in Florida, teaching a weeklong course for Master's International Divinity School. Shortly after that, the next year's Women of Faith schedule would resume, and I'd be happily back to normal (or as normal as I ever was) and on my way through a productive and rewarding year without any of the health problems that had necessitated the surgery.

That was my plan. Once I announced to my doctor and the world in general what I would do, the prayer chains were activated. I fervently prayed that God would give me strength and courage to face this little procedure. I confidently headed off to the hospital on December 8, after telling my friends and family I wasn't worried in the least.

Looking back, I now identify even more strongly with the woman who reached out to Jesus that day so long ago. Although she had suffered her physical problems for years longer than I'd had to deal with mine, we both believed the same thing: *Jesus could heal us.* So we both headed out the door of our homes with hope in our hearts and conviction in our faith.

I came through that surgery without a hitch and woke up that afternoon feeling fine and feisty—well, except for that big incision stapled shut across my tummy. It slowed me down a little, but otherwise, I was my regular sweet, docile, and undemanding self. "I want *food!*" I announced. "Give me something to eat!"

And here they came with Jell-O, apple juice, and something they called broth. Well, that made me a little cranky. I said, "Y'all, this ain't food! I need more than this. I'm hungry!"

They said, "You can have all the broth you want."

Somehow I survived the all-liquid diet and set my mind on recovering, but as the hours passed, I sensed something was wrong. However much I wanted to go home, when the doctor said I could be discharged on December 11, I told the hospital staff I didn't think I was ready.

"Oh, you just need to get home and get rested," the nurse told me. "Surgery takes a lot out of you. You don't have a fever, and your body functions are normal, so you're definitely ready to go. Anyway, you can catch more diseases in the hospital than almost anywhere else. You're much better off at home than you are here."

So home I went, ready to get well and live out the happy ending I'd envisioned for this little surgical story. Although, I now had twinges of doubt about how quickly I could recover, since I was still in quite a bit of pain. But I trusted my doctor and I trusted God. Between the two of them, I knew my healing would happen.

After all, that was my plan.

She Knew Jesus Could Heal

I imagine that woman who reached out to Jesus also had a plan when she left her home that morning. Maybe she pictured herself walking up and sitting down beside Him in some peaceful setting, perhaps while He was taking a lunch break. She could quietly and discreetly explain her embarrassing request. Maybe she thought He would rest His hands on her head and pray for her.

All that's just a guess. But there's one thing concerning this woman that I'm certain about: *She knew Jesus could heal her.*

She might even have had plans for what to do that afternoon once her health was restored. Maybe she intended to stop by a girlfriend's house on the way home and share her good news. Or maybe, like me, she was planning to host a family event in a few days, and she looked forward to doing so without the pain, exhaustion, and general distractions she'd endured over such a long time of illness.

Whatever the case, I picture her heading out confidently, knowing her life was about to change for the better. I imagine her hurrying down the road or through the streets, following her plan to find Jesus and speak to Him. Maybe a distant roar of voices or a billowing cloud of dust was her first indication there might be a hitch in her plan. She hadn't counted on seeing what Mark calls "a great crowd" (Mark

5:24). Did she question whether everything would go as easy as she'd hoped? If she'd been counting on an opportunity to approach Jesus quietly, she must have finally let go of that plan as she got caught up in that swirling horde of humanity.

She must have squeezed her way through that surging mob...or perhaps she was just swept along. Somehow she reached Him. And then, once there, did she trip or fall? Or perhaps she simply collapsed from her weakened state and the exhausting ordeal. Whatever happened, she ended up right behind Him, but down low—low enough to touch the hem of His cloak. And her hand reached out...

However crushed her expectations, she hadn't given up, and her unfaltering faith made that enough. She was immediately healed.

When Our Plans Get Knocked Down

A few days after I came home from the hospital, I had a bad coughing spell. Usually if I had to cough or sneeze, I would hold a cushion over my tummy to keep from straining the surgical incision. But this time the coughing fit hit me when no cushion was near. I coughed and coughed and coughed without the familiar shock absorber. Afterward I felt as if little fish were swimming around in my stomach.

I called the doctor's office. The nurse asked me several questions, and then she assured me everything sounded normal. But when I went back for the follow-up exam later that week, the doctor was shocked to see that I had an infection. He prescribed antibiotics, and I returned home and went back to bed, groaning from the ever-increasing pain.

My expectations were not finding fulfillment. My plan had developed a kink. And I was about to get knocked down.

That night my incision split open, and I saw parts of myself I never wanted to see. I'm so grateful that my husband, George, and my daughter Vikki were with me when it happened. I was in such misery I couldn't have coped on my own. They called 9-1-1, but more problems kept crowding around me, kicking and shoving. When the paramedics arrived, their gurney was too wide to fit through the door. They had to sit me up on a chair and carry me outside. It was an excruciating ordeal. With my incision gaping open and my insides bulging out, the pain was overwhelming.

This Is Victory?

I can guess what you're thinking:

> *Thelma, what kind of "victory over depression story" is this? I picked up this book thinking it would lift my spirits, but you're describing something that makes me want to lose my lunch!*

Let me continue.

It's true that sometimes when we need God most we feel far away from Him—hurting, alone, forgotten, trampled down by a crowd of problems. Maybe at that point we've given up on ever feeling close to Him again. Maybe we feel dirty and unfit, covered with worldly dust that robs us of courage and weakens our faith.

No wonder we get depressed.

Well, let me tell you: When you find yourself that low, remember the woman who reached out through the mob to touch the hem of her Savior's cloak. There may have been something in her that wanted to think He had passed her by or forgotten her or turned His back on her. The devil's been wanting us all to think that for a long, long time. Ah, but she knew better. She knew that even if she didn't feel close to Jesus, even if she couldn't look Him in the eye and talk to Him face-to-face, *He* still knew who she was and what her situation was.

I was knocked down by blinding pain that night, horrified by what was happening and feeling far from God as the paramedics finally loaded me into the ambulance and set off for the hospital with the red lights flashing. That was a very unfamiliar place for Thelma Wells to be. And I'm not just talking about being in the back of the ambulance. I'm also talking about feeling far from God. To explain, let me tell a little of what had already happened between God and me.

Getting Close Again

I grew up in church. I was reared by my great-grandparents, and for most of my growing-up years, "Granny" was in church every day, and I went with her. Monday we went to missions meeting. Tuesday was women's auxiliary. Wednesday was prayer meeting. Thursday we attended choir rehearsal. Friday was the teachers' meeting. We helped clean the church on Saturdays, and we were back bright and early Sunday mornings.

I guess I thought I knew everything there was to know about God and the church because when I got to college, I got a little bored and stopped attending services. I had more urgent things to do, such as study and sleep…and eventually date George. Then George and I got married, and Sunday morning was the only time we had to spend together—just the two of us—so we stayed home.

I never stopped believing—goodness no! And I never stopped praying and studying my Bible. But I drifted away from the close relationship I'd always had with God.

This had been going on a few years, when one day I encountered a friend from church who told me a new women's class was being organized. She not only invited me to attend, she asked me to teach it. She said, "You used to teach, and it was such a wonderful experience, Thelma. I just know you're supposed to come back and teach this class."

I wanted to say, "I just know you're supposed to get out of my face." But over the next month I kept running into this woman. She seemed to turn up everywhere I went. Here's a summary of our long-running dialogue:

"Will you teach the class?"

"No!"

"Will you teach the class?"

"No!"

"Will you teach the class?

"Okay."

Once I agreed to start teaching, I got back into intensely researching the Word and praying, and it was like eating a piece of chocolate after being on a decades-long diet. I couldn't get enough! I taught that

Bible class for 10 years, and through that work I became closer than ever to my heavenly Father.

Couldn't Take Any More

Not only was my faith renewed and strengthened by studying God's Word, but I also saw it manifested right before my eyes. I learned all over again that Jesus is the Healer, the Miracle Worker, the glorious and omnipotent Lord God Almighty, and the same yesterday, today, and forever.

At one point, a young woman in the church had leukemia, and she was scheduled to undergo an emergency procedure in the hospital on a Sunday morning. Her mother called the church during Sunday school and asked us to stop and pray for her daughter before the procedure began, and we did exactly that. Later that morning, before the sermon began, the mother called again, crazy with joy. She said, "While you all were praying, they came in to give her one last test before starting the procedure—and her blood is perfect. They're discharging her. We're leaving the hospital!"

That young woman has not had one symptom of leukemia since that day! Her good health is the manifestation of Jehovah God, who is the Healer. *God can heal us.* I've seen Him do it, and each time I've watched a miracle unfold, my faith has grown stronger. I live to love and praise Him, and I have felt His powerful presence in my life with every breath I take.

Back in the Ambulance

But getting back to my story, there I was…in the back of an ambulance, pain totally consuming me. I felt far away from God the Healer, God the Miracle Worker, God my loving Father. The paramedic who was tending to me as we rushed to the hospital swabbed my arm with something cold, and I begged him, "Please, don't try to find a vein. Please. No more pain! No more! *Please…*" I struggled to fling out one more prayer through the pain—maybe in the same way that woman in biblical times had stretched out her arm through the crowd, thinking, *Oh, Jesus, please. No more. I can't take any more!*

Then miraculously, before the words had even left my heart, I fell asleep, and the pain ended. I don't remember anything else that happened until 24 hours later…sometime the next evening.

When I remember that loud and tortuous ambulance ride, and how Jesus gave me relief, I can't help but think, *Who wouldn't serve a Savior like that?*

I Love Him More

You see, I know something that the woman who touched the Lord's cloak *couldn't* know…because it hadn't happened yet.

After my ordeal, I believe I know just a smidgen—just a morsel, just the tiniest bit—of what Jesus went through when He hung on that cross to die for me. In my own insignificant way, I have a better understanding now of the agony He must have felt when He cried out, "My God, my God, why have you forsaken me?" (Matthew 27:46). When I look at the pain and torture He endured for my sake, and then consider the momentary light affliction I went through, I love Him more than ever.

I thought I really loved Jesus before, but now I love Him more. *I love Him more!*

And only now do I believe that my faith comes anywhere close to the amazing faith of that woman who knew without a doubt—even before Jesus' crucifixion and the resurrection that were still to come—that He could heal her—even if she merely touched the hem of His cloak.

How thankful I am that she knew what she knew—and that her story has been handed down to me these 2000 years later.

Good News in Our Journey Together

Everybody enjoys hearing good news, right? Men, women, boys, and girls—we're all looking for good news about hope, joy, peace, contentment, patience, gentleness, and kindness. Everybody wants *practical* ways to deal with negative issues. We *all* need that kind of help. And what do we especially need? *Biblical* ways to deal with difficulties, including depression.

Do you still have in mind the woman reaching out to touch the hem of Jesus' garment? Well, when you and I reach out toward Him, we have something even better to lay hold of! We have the written Word of God.

That's why I hope you'll read your Bible regularly as we journey together. We'll be thinking about and responding to some very helpful scriptures throughout this trip.

If you're in the depths of depression, maybe you're thinking, *I've tried looking at verses, and that isn't really helping me right now.* That's okay. I've been there too. Everyone, at times, needs help and encouragement in getting into and understanding God's Word. So I warmly invite you to please look to God's Word again. Let me strongly encourage you to get out your Bible, and as you do, remember this exciting promise: "The law of the LORD is perfect, *reviving the soul*" (Psalm 19:7).

When you think about it, isn't it amazing that even when we're at the end of our resources, we still so often drag our feet about going to God for help—the only One ultimately who can truly help us? But even more amazing is how God truly *understands* our resistance and narrow-sightedness. After all, He sent His Son Jesus to die for those things on our behalf. And Jesus keeps coming to us in mercy to lift us beyond our limitations.

Open Your Heart and Mind

I pray that you'll open your heart, open your mind, and receive God's words that can help you heal and give you the strength and encouragement you need to deal with your situation. In fact, why wait? Grab a pen and paper (or journal) and your Bible. Read the amazing story we've been discussing in Luke 8:43-48:

> [43]And there was a woman who had had a discharge of blood for twelve years, and though she had spent all her living on physicians, she could not be healed by anyone. [44]She came up behind him and touched the fringe of his garment, and immediately her discharge of blood ceased. [45]And Jesus said, "Who was it that touched me?" When all denied it, Peter said, "Master, the crowds surround you

and are pressing in on you!" ⁴⁶But Jesus said, "Someone touched me, for I perceive that power has gone out from me." ⁴⁷And when the woman saw that she was not hidden, she came trembling, and falling down before him declared in the presence of all the people why she had touched him, and how she had been immediately healed. ⁴⁸And he said to her, "Daughter, your faith has made you well; go in peace."

❀ Read verse 47 again and imagine yourself standing with her in that situation. Briefly record your impressions from the woman based on that verse—her posture, her actions, her statements. Include what stands out to you about her.

This woman is still down low, but there is much that has now changed in her situation, isn't there?

❀ Now approach verse 48 in the same way. What are your impressions from the response that Jesus gave to this woman? What's the most significant thing that stands out to you about what He told her?

Let these words from Jesus continue to ring in your mind as you proceed through this book.

God Will Help You!

I can't guarantee that by going through this book you'll experience a breakthrough in your difficult circumstances. But I believe you can and will experience a breakthrough in your heart and mind...and that this will eventually free up your vision to finally see the true solutions to your situation. And I believe that after working through this book with "an honest and good heart" (Luke 8:15), you will surely catch sight of the divine strength that will lift you out of depression so you can experience God's wonderful, fully satisfying peace.

1

The Truth About Depression

We're going to explore some practical, biblical ways to deal with depression. But first, what exactly is depression? If we've been sad for a long while, is that the same as being depressed? After all, most people don't mind so much if other people think we look a little sad. But if people assume we must be *depressed*, that's often a different matter entirely, isn't it?

Some people perceive a stigma associated with depression, so they're quite reluctant to admit they're depressed. This means they don't openly deal with it or seek help. They suppose everybody else is always upbeat and positive, so they must be the only one who's mixed up or feeling down.

Christians in particular are often afraid to acknowledge depression because they associate it with a spiritual breakdown or weakness. And this is despite knowing that several of our biblical heroes extolled in the pages of Scripture definitely showed evidence of depression.

I'm sure you know by now that believing in the Lord Jesus Christ doesn't mean all your problems are history. The fact is, depression is extremely common. At some point in our lives, almost all of us will either face a significant encounter with depression or see a family member or close friend struggle with it. Psychologists estimate that 20 percent of adults will experience *severe* depression at some point in their lives, and many of them more than once.

The most acute cases of depression, known as "clinical depression," require professional help. Please don't hesitate to see a counselor or physician if you recognize symptoms of severe depression in your life.

Although depression appears to be as old as humanity, there are indications that it's growing more common today than in previous generations. Why is that? Here's a disturbing explanation from Dr. Archibald D. Hart, a leading Christian psychologist and dean emeritus of the School of Psychology at Fuller Theological Seminary:

> The frantic pace of modern life combined with a breakdown of traditional values is causing many to feel hopeless, uncertain and disappointed. This stress aggravates the genetic factors that predispose to biological depressions. It also sets the stage for an appalling sense of loss, which is the primary cause of psychological depressions. Demoralization is rampant in our modern culture and can turn an even minor setback into a major depression in a body overextended by stress.
>
> Many losses in our modern world are tangible and material. More significant, however, in causing psychological depression are such losses as insecurity, uncertainty, rejection, lack of fulfillment in one's vocation, and a general sense of the meaninglessness of life. These are losses that were not as prevalent in earlier times. As a culture, we may well have entered our own emotional "Great Depression."[1]

Notice what Dr. Hart said about *loss* as something that brings on depression. All of us experience our share of losses, don't we? We'll look more carefully at this in just a moment.

Who Gets Depressed?

Dr. Hart also observes that depression "is found with frightening regularity in ourselves, our relatives and our friends. There is hardly a family today that is not touched by depression's tentacles."[2] Depression affects people of all social classes, all races, and all cultures, but there's one group that's especially hard hit. Again Dr. Hart explains:

Women…are significantly at greater risk for depression than men (a two to one ratio). The reasons for this are twofold.

First, the reproductive biochemistry of the female body implicates depression more often. At various times during the menstrual cycle, as well as in the life cycle of reproduction, depression results from hormonal changes. Problems with depression just before menstruation (premenstrual syndrome) as well as later in life (menopausal depression) are extremely common.

Second, it is very clear that women today are under greater stress than men. Mothers often have to work a full-time job in addition to taking care of family needs. Their resources for coping are therefore pushed to the limits. The result is a greater propensity toward fatigue and depressions caused by adrenaline exhaustion.[3]

Dr. Hart also writes, "We are seeing an alarming increase in childhood depressions. In fact, the dramatic increase in depression in both the very young and the elderly is among the most frightening features of modern-day depression."[4]

Isn't this tragic? I've been made aware especially of the growing prevalence of depression among teenagers. I asked my friend Freda McKissic Bush, MD, to give us some of her insights about depression, especially regarding teens:

"Alice," a 19-year-old college student, came to me for a consultation because she'd missed her menstrual cycles after having been sexually active with her boyfriend until three months ago. Because she had gained weight and was sleeping more than normal, she thought she might be pregnant. A pregnancy test showed she was not.

As I completed her medical history and physical examination, she asked, "When will I get over having that abortion last year? I cry myself to sleep every night." She wondered if the abortion had made her unable to get pregnant.

She said that besides breaking up with her boyfriend, her relations with her mother were strained, she had difficulty making decisions, she was doing poorly in school, and generally felt anxious and miserable. Although she denied having made plans for suicide, she admitted thinking she would be better off dead.

Alice showed classic signs of depression. Despite the medical reasons for her irregular cycles, the psychological ones could not be overlooked.

Depression affects all aspects of a person—body, mind, and spirit. It can happen to anyone, and it can happen at any age. However, statistics show that both boys and girls experimenting with sex were three times more likely to have symptoms of depression than their friends who have never had sex…Research indicates that sexually active girls ages 12 to 16 were over three times more likely to have attempted suicide as their virgin friends, while sexually active boys were eight times more likely to attempt suicide.[5] Suicide is the third leading cause of death among adolescents ages 15 to 19.

Meanwhile, subsequent conversations and referral for counseling helped Alice recognize that some of her symptoms could be caused by her sexual behavior.

If you have had sex, you can choose to stop and wait until marriage to have sex again. The benefits are that you can regain your self-respect, reduce your risk for depression, and improve your success at a healthy lifestyle.

In our culture today, we all need to be increasingly aware of the many forces that are increasingly pushing people of every age over the edge of depression.[6]

Triggers…and Treatment

What causes depression? *Psychology Information Online,* which includes content provided by the National Institute on Mental Health, notes that "a depressive episode" can be triggered by "a serious loss, chronic illness, relationship problems, work stress, family crisis, financial setback, or any unwelcome life change." Whatever the cause of our depression, it needs to be faced and understood realistically—and then accepted for what it truly is.

Sometimes depression is brought on by an underlying disease or biochemical disorder. Fortunately, the medical field has made significant strides both in identifying these causes and in developing effective treatments for them. When it comes to taking antidepressants, Dr. Hart emphasizes that these "have far fewer side effects than earlier ones and are perfectly safe when taken under supervision for long periods of time." He also notes that these newer medications "are not addicting. They may be taken without fear of becoming dependent on them."

Psychology Information Online makes this point: "As a general rule, you should never take antidepressant medication alone, without also beginning psychotherapy, or at least seeing a psychologist for an evaluation."[7]

Furthermore, Dr. Hart notes that "there is no medication to speak of" for treating the more common cases of situational depression (which he terms "reactive depression"). This kind of situational depression usually involves the loss of something significant. Following such a loss, the depression we experience "is essentially a call to let go of whatever it is we have lost." Dr. Hart continues:

> God has designed us for grief, so that whether the loss is the death of a loved one, the departure of our first child to college, getting fired from a job, or a business venture that has gone bad, we have to face this loss with courage and allow ourselves to grieve...This is what reactive depression is all about. It is a healing time to help us cope with loss.[8]

❦ Have you experienced a significant loss recently? Or if you experienced a loss not so recently, is it still affecting you? Write down what you lost and when.

✿ Now write down how that loss is affecting you emotionally. Also include any other ways it's affecting you. Have the effects changed over time?

Do you remember the words of Ecclesiastes 3:1? "For everything there is a season, and a time for every matter under heaven." That includes "*a time to heal*...and a time to laugh; *a time to mourn,* and a time to dance" (verses 3 and 4). If you've experienced a significant loss that's still affecting you, you may still be in the "time to mourn," which is entirely appropriate and natural. Remember to give yourself time to heal. If you try to rush the process, suppress it, or take shortcuts, the emotions will eventually burst out...often in harmful ways.

✿ If you're still in that time of grieving over a loss, talk to God about it. Ask Him to be with you and to heal you. Ask Him to be part of your grieving process. He wants to help! Write down what you want to tell Him about your situation.

✿ Who else can you talk to about this?

Less Severe Depression

Some of us are more prone to depression than others. The influences that bring us down in our spirits can come from many sources and directions. Depression can be a complex picture. But let's face it. The main reason we get despondent is simply because *life happens.* And nobody's life is a constant procession of uplifting, rejuvenating, invigorating experiences. Everybody's life has downers. We easily get off-balance in so many ways, and this hurts.

For most of us, the depression we typically encounter isn't in the severe category, medically speaking. The typical depression is *situational.* This doesn't mean they're painless or less important or harmless. Dr. Hart writes, "While these depressions are not usually as serious as the biological ones, they can be much more difficult to cope with." He goes on to say,

> One of the most unfortunate secondary effects of depression is that it often causes the sufferer to be oblivious to the depression. Depression eludes recognition, especially in the less severe types. Some people can be depressed for a long time, therefore, and not realize it. Depression can also mask itself in irritability, fatigue, and workaholism. Many who overeat do so as a form of "self-medication" to ease their dejected state. Even when someone vaguely knows he or she is depressed, there is a tendency to deny the depression. Depression is often mistakenly viewed as a weakness, and people fear that even acknowledging their emotional pain to themselves is an admission of defeat.[9]

So we need to be sensitive to our condition and be able to identify the symptoms of depression. What are those symptoms?

Fatigue is certainly a common and prominent symptom, but many others have been identified as well. *Psychology Information Online* notes that depression's symptoms "may vary from person to person, and also depend on the severity of the depression." It lists a very wide range of symptoms, and summarizes them in the following four areas. (As you read, underline any words or phrases that describe you right now.)

- *Changes in Thinking*—You may experience problems with concentration and decision making. Some people report difficulty with short-term memory, forgetting things all the time. Negative thoughts are characteristic of depression. Pessimism, poor self-esteem, excessive guilt, and self-criticism are all common. Some people have self-destructive thoughts during a more serious depression.

- *Changes in Feelings*—You may feel sad for no reason at all. Some people report that they no longer enjoy activities that they once found pleasurable. You might lack motivation and become more apathetic. You might feel "slowed down" and tired all the time. Sometimes irritability is a problem, and you may have more difficulty controlling your temper. In the extreme, depression is characterized by feelings of helplessness and hopelessness.

- *Changes in Behavior*—Changes in behavior during depression are reflective of the negative emotions being experienced. You might act more apathetic because that's how you feel. Some people do not feel comfortable with other people, so social withdrawal is common. You may experience a dramatic change in appetite, either eating more or less. Because of the chronic sadness, excessive crying is common. Some people complain about everything and act out their anger with temper outbursts. Sexual desire may disappear, resulting in lack of sexual activity. In the extreme, people may neglect their personal appearance, even neglecting basic hygiene. Needless to say, someone who is this depressed does not do very much, so work productivity and household responsibilities suffer. Some people even have trouble getting out of bed.

- *Changes in Physical Well-being*—Negative emotional feelings experienced during depression are coupled with negative physical emotions as well. Chronic fatigue, despite spending more time sleeping, is common. Some people can't sleep, or don't sleep soundly. These individuals lay awake for hours, or awaken many times during the night, and stare at the ceiling. Others sleep many hours, even most of the day, although they still feel tired. Many people lose their appetite, feel slowed down by depression, and complain of many aches and pains. Others are restless and can't sit still.[10]

Did you underline anything? If you did, it's time to pay attention to what you've noticed and seek help by talking to someone about the issues raised. I suggest you also find out if what you're experiencing has a physical cause, such as a hormonal or brain chemistry imbalance. Ask God to give you wisdom regarding how to move forward toward healing and peace...and then do it!

I often receive letters from people who are depressed that really grab me. Many include statements like these:

- Thelma, I feel like I'm losing my mind.

- Life is just too hard. I want out of here now.

- People are cruel to me.

- Nothing goes right for me.

- I can't think straight.

- I can't stop crying.

- Nothing brings me pleasure.

- My family doesn't even want to have anything to do with me.

- I can't keep relationships.

- When I talk to my friends, they tell me I need to see a counselor. I am not going to see a counselor 'cause I've seen a counselor, and it's the counselor who needs to be on the couch.

- I refuse to take medication. I absolutely refuse.

- I have to force myself out of the house.

- I just want to sleep my life away.

- Nobody cares anyway. I don't even think you care. You probably think I'm crazy.

- Help!

There are a number of reasons why people get depressed, and you may identify with much of what you just read. But let me assure you of one important thing: *You are not crazy.* Don't even think you might be crazy.

For the rest of this book we're going to specifically address situational depression, although the truths that we'll look at from Scripture will be rewarding and helpful for every one of us, even if the depression is primarily due to physical causes and biochemical imbalances. Again, I encourage you to seek professional help from a counselor or physician if you believe you might be battling severe depression.

Now, I don't want to lay a guilt trip on you. I certainly don't want to make your despondency any greater than it already is. But don't we sometimes make things worse by our responses to life's downers? We might even throw ourselves a pity party and say, "I *deserve* to be depressed. Just look at what all I've been through!" We will discover how to respond to situations in a better way. In the next chapter, we'll continue to keep thinking this through. As we do, let's open our hearts to the wisdom found in the Word of God.

2

Looking for Peace

Remember those uplifting words Jesus spoke to the woman who'd touched His garment? As she knelt down before Him, He said, "Daughter, your faith has made you well; go in peace" (Luke 8:48). I think He must have said that because she'd been deprived of peace for so long because of her condition.

You can be sorrowful...yet still be at peace. You can be weary... and still be at peace. You can even be grieving...and still experience peace. But *depression* and experiencing God's peace never seem to go together. And this is all the more tragic because depression very often is not caused by any moral failing or any sin against God, and yet it keeps us from enjoying His peace. It's like a heavy cloud cover that blocks the sweet, fresh air of God's peace.

I know there are moments or even seasons in life when we tend to lose our connection with God's peace. But that doesn't rule out the higher reality that God wants us to know and enjoy His peace. In fact, He intends for us to live in that peace day by day:

> Peace I leave with you; my peace I give to you. Not as the
> world gives do I give to you. Let not your hearts be troubled,
> neither let them be afraid (John 14:27 ESV).

✸ What did the Lord Jesus promise His followers regarding His peace?

✸ When you're truly at peace, you feel secure. What most often threatens your sense of security in the Lord? Do you recognize any patterns in your life in this regard?

Perhaps in times when you've experienced depression, they began with times of sorrow, tears, and hurts. If that's true, there's a promise from God for you in Isaiah 25:8-9:

> He will swallow up death forever;
> and the Lord GOD will wipe away tears from all faces,
> and the reproach of his people he will take away from all
>   the earth,
> for the LORD has spoken.
> It will be said on that day,
> "Behold, this is our God; we have waited for him, that he
>   might save us.
> This is the LORD; we have waited for him;
> let us be glad and rejoice in his salvation."

✸ God wants you to know this promise well, so why not memorize it this week? To help you remember the promise, write it down in your own words:

Wanting What's Good

In the depths of situational depression, we long for something good...or something better. In fact, if these desires weren't inside us, we wouldn't have anything to be depressed about. So even when you're down, recognize this reality. Remind yourself of this often. In fact, copy this statement down and post it in several places where you'll see it often:

> *I still desire to experience what is good*
> *and right and whole in my life.*

Embrace those desires in a new way and with a new passion.

❊ What are your strongest and deepest desires for what is good and right?

❊ How does God view those desires? Didn't He, in fact, place them inside you? And isn't He ultimately responsible to fulfill them? What do you think?

So the question for your future, as far as God's involvement goes, is, "Will God fulfill my legitimate desires?" And what are "legitimate desires"? It's when your desires are based in your goal to delight in the Lord:

> Delight yourself in the LORD,
> and he will give you the desires of your heart.

Commit your way to the LORD;
    trust in him, and he will act
(Psalm 37:4-5).

⚜ How do your desires stack up against Psalm 37:4-5's teachings?

⚜ If you are indeed delighting yourself in the Lord, is it possible to be depressed?

On the Way

If we were looking at reality with perfect, God-given vision, the only people in despair would be those who refuse to believe in Christ. Despair is a truly appropriate (and tragic) response for people who refuse to accept the love Christ offers and the sacrifice He made so they could be with Him forever. For those whose destination is heaven through Christ, we are on our way toward experiencing complete joy in eternity. So why would we get depressed? Because we're not there yet! We're still *on the way*. We're *in process* of growing in the Lord. We've got our destination planned, but we must complete the journey God has for us.

⚜ What are some clear evidences in your life and experiences that demonstrate you're still on the way to spiritual maturity and total joy in the Lord?

❀ In your personality, mindset, and habits, do you think of yourself as someone who's "in process"? Are you someone who's still "on the way" to becoming all that God has designed and gifted you to be? Or do you see yourself as stuck, as pretty much the person you'll be in this life?

Down deep, some believers think they'll *never* be perfect. But this notion is just as wrong as assuming we don't have anything to learn. Both these misconceptions are rooted in pride—a pride that blocks out or distorts the truth God tells us in His Word. Our perfection is in Jesus Christ. Through Him we are "holy and blameless" in God's sight (Ephesians 1:4).

❀ Mark where you see yourself on the scale (0 = I don't expect any significant change in who I am; 10 = I'm expecting complete transformation in who I am).

0   1   2   3   4   5   6   7   8   9   10

If you and I had the gifting and the experiences of the apostle Paul, we would probably think we'd pretty much *arrived* in the Christian life. But Paul, even though he was an apostle, recognized that he was *in process*. And that process was *intense*. Just look at Philippians 3:7-16, especially verses 12-16:

> ⁷Whatever gain I had, I counted as loss for the sake of Christ. ⁸Indeed, I count everything as loss because of the surpassing worth of knowing Christ Jesus my Lord. For his sake I have suffered the loss of all things and count them as rubbish, in order that I may gain Christ ⁹and be found in him, not having a righteousness of my own that comes from the law, but that which comes through faith

in Christ, the righteousness from God that depends on faith—[10]that I may know him and the power of his resurrection, and may share his sufferings, becoming like him in his death, [11]that by any means possible I may attain the resurrection from the dead.

[12]Not that I have already obtained this or am already perfect, but I press on to make it my own, because Christ Jesus has made me his own. [13]Brothers, I do not consider that I have made it my own. But one thing I do: forgetting what lies behind and straining forward to what lies ahead, [14]I press on toward the goal for the prize of the upward call of God in Christ Jesus. [15]Let those of us who are mature think this way, and if in anything you think otherwise, God will reveal that also to you. [16]Only let us hold true to what we have attained (Philippians 3:7-16).

⊗ Notice in verse 12 that Paul's attitude is based on his sense of belonging. Who does Paul say he belongs to...and why?

> *"Progress is process leading to success."*
> THELMA WELLS

To know simply that we belong to the Lord—that we are *His* responsibility, that we are totally *His* to watch over and care for—brings us peace and freedom *and* a reason to press on!

⊗ In your experience (past and present), what has given you the strongest motivation to "press on" in life?

✿ At this moment, how strong is your personal sense of belonging to the Lord? Mark your answer on the scale (0 = I don't feel like I'm part of His family or that He cares about me; 10 = He's the total source of my identity and security).

0   1   2   3   4   5   6   7   8   9   10

✿ In the Philippians passage you just looked at, Paul graciously tells us about his mindset.

❀ How did he view his past?

❀ How did he view his future?

✿ Now, if you were writing instead of Paul, what would your perspective on your past and future be? Complete the following statements.

❀ Regarding what lies behind, I...

❀ Regarding what lies ahead, I...

❧ According to Philippians 3:14, as Paul was nearing the end of his days on earth, what target was he aiming for?

❧ What parts of his statement are true for you?

❧ Put the parts of Paul's statement that fit you in your words for your life today.

❧ Is it hard for you to think the same way Paul does about life? If yes, that's probably true for just about all of us! So what gracious promise from God can we count on, according to verse 15?

When You're Downcast

Paul described our loving Father as "God, who *comforts the downcast*" (2 Corinthians 7:6). Let's explore the dynamics of that, okay?

Psalms 42 and 43 together represent the cry of a downcast soul—someone who is hurting and thirsting for God. Take a moment and quietly reflect on Psalm 42:5 (which is repeated in 42:11 and 43:5):

> Why are you cast down, O my soul,
>   and why are you in turmoil within me?
> Hope in God; for I shall again praise him,
>   my salvation.

The big question this person is asking is, "Why?" And when we're depressed, we ask this too because it's often hard to identify the reason for our sorrow. The writer of these two psalms didn't understand the reason for the trouble in his soul that was dragging him down. But he did know this condition had to be temporary. How do we know this? What did the psalmist command himself to do in Psalm 42:5? He told himself to "hope in God." And what was his reason? "For I shall again praise him, my salvation."

Does this really work? When you're downcast or depressed, is it possible to order yourself to "hope in God," and then just do it? And if you do, will that automatically pull you into peace and happiness? Think about these questions as you stop and read Psalm 42 and 43. Note how this process worked for the psalm writer.

Psalm 42

> As a deer pants for flowing streams,
>   so pants my soul for you, O God.
> My soul thirsts for God,
>   for the living God.
> When shall I come and appear before God?
> My tears have been my food
>   day and night, while they say to me continually,
>   "Where is your God?"
> These things I remember,
>   as I pour out my soul:
>   how I would go with the throng
>   and lead them in procession to the house of God

with glad shouts and songs of praise,
    a multitude keeping festival.
Why are you cast down, O my soul,
    and why are you in turmoil within me?
Hope in God; for I shall again praise him,
    my salvation and my God.

My soul is cast down within me;
    therefore I remember you
    from the land of Jordan and of Hermon,
    from Mount Mizar.
Deep calls to deep
    at the roar of your waterfalls;
    all your breakers and your waves
    have gone over me.
By day the LORD commands his steadfast love,
    and at night his song is with me,
    a prayer to the God of my life.
I say to God, my rock:
    "Why have you forgotten me?
    Why do I go mourning
    because of the oppression of the enemy?"
As with a deadly wound in my bones,
    my adversaries taunt me,
    while they say to me continually,
    "Where is your God?"
Why are you cast down, O my soul,
    and why are you in turmoil within me?
Hope in God; for I shall again praise him,
    my salvation and my God.

PSALM 43

Vindicate me, O God, and defend my cause
    against an ungodly people,
from the deceitful and unjust man
    deliver me!
For you are the God in whom I take refuge;
    why have you rejected me?

Why do I go about mourning
    because of the oppression of the enemy?
Send out your light and your truth;
    let them lead me;
let them bring me to your holy hill
    and to your dwelling!
Then I will go to the altar of God,
    to God my exceeding joy,
and I will praise you with the lyre,
    O God, my God.

Why are you cast down, O my soul,
    and why are you in turmoil within me?
Hope in God; for I shall again praise him,
    my salvation and my God.

The psalmist expressed his depression and then summed up the results by declaring that hope in God is the cure for despair. To gain hope we must surrender our emotions to God through faith and trust in Him. He will fulfill His every promise to love, care, and watch over us.

  ✿ According to the psalms you just read, how can you deliberately "hope in God"?

  ✿ What do you see in these psalms that indicates this person's humility before God?

❀ What do you see that indicates his deep love for God and his enjoyment of God?

When it comes to moving ourselves out of depression and into encouragement and joy, these psalms show a balance by revealing actions we take and actions God takes.

❀ What actions do we need to take?

❀ What actions do we need to let God handle?

❀ What are the most significant things you've learned about depression in this chapter?

3

Taking Action

My friend Sheila Walsh says, "It's hard for me to describe to you what it's like if you've never suffered from depression. It feels as if *a cold winter is settling on your soul.*" If you feel that cold winter wind howling around you (or you know someone close to you is feeling it), I want to help you step forward into the warm breezes of springtime.

We're going to look at four ways of addressing depression. Even if you've never experienced "significant" depression, it's very likely that a time will come when you'll find great help from understanding these four things—not to mention being better able to understand and be of service to people you know who might be depressed.

Are you ready to win over depression? Let's get started!

Get It All Out

The first thing I encourage you to do is *talk to somebody* about how you're feeling. Emotionally and mentally, talking about your feelings is a healthy thing for you to do. Everybody needs somebody to confide in. That's right. *Everybody.*

We also need someone who will hear our questions and concerns and then respond in a helpful manner. So carefully consider who you can share with. You want someone who is safe, discreet, and has *godly wisdom* to offer. Don't go to just anybody. Everyone has an opinion he or she is willing to give you, but opinions can be negative, fault-finding, not helpful, destructive, and confusing. So when you choose someone, make sure the person dives into God's Word regularly. Talk to someone who will draw on the Word and share the Word when responding to you. Choose someone who will pray with you and help you find answers for yourself in the Word.

There are still other issues you need to talk about. You see, a lot of depression is caused by keeping negative emotions inside us. A lot of it is *anger* we've accumulated or felt that is directed at specific people. Whoever and whatever you're angry about, you need to do something about it. Did you know that? Is that what you were afraid of? Well, what you *don't* need is to keep holding those bad feelings inside. And no, this doesn't mean you get to or have to explode at someone.

I suggest you get pen and paper and write letters to the people with whom you're angry. Even if they're not alive or in your life anymore, write to them. In your letters say *everything* that's on your mind. I encourage you to include the vulgar stuff, the stupid stuff, the surprising stuff you may not even know is inside you. All the hatred, the malice, the frustration, the disappointment—get it all out in writing.

What's next? *Do not mail that letter!* And if you still sense anger inside, write another letter. *Don't mail that one either.* Keep writing letters as long as the anger's there. You may need a big legal pad. You may need lots of pens and pencils. You may need reams of computer paper. Whatever it takes, get your emotions out.

Now, maybe you don't want to write down any of this. Maybe you think you're not good at expressing yourself in writing. Talk to a chair then. Put a paper bag on the chair, write the person's name on it, and start talking. Tell him or her exactly what you think. But make sure you're alone...and that nobody's listening—especially not the person represented by the paper bag. (After all, if we told people *everything* we thought about them, we wouldn't have any friends, would we? Our feelings are changing constantly, and our hearts are deceitful and sometimes only reveal the surface emotions [Mark 7:21; Romans 1:21; 1 Corinthians 4:5].)

The point is to find some healthy way of *venting* that doesn't cause harm. Get the poisonous anger into the light of day and then out of your system. This will help start the healing process.

   ✽ Who will you talk to…and when?

   ✽ I encourage you to take a moment and write down your plan for talking with somebody about what you're going through. Be as brief or as detailed about this plan as you want to be, but put something down in writing that will help you be committed to following through.

Take Care of Yourself Physically

Next I encourage you to make sure you *take care of yourself physically*. Now, you've heard that line often enough already, haven't you? Sure you have. But are you *doing* it? That's the bottom line.

I can't emphasize enough how important this is, especially when we're struggling with depression because that's when we're most likely to let go of good habits for our physical well-being. And how healthy we are physically always impacts our mental, emotional, and spiritual health.

There's a great deal of information that could be included on this topic, and you may be someone who needs to hear every bit of it. Or you may be someone who's heard it all already, but you haven't taken heed. Whatever your situation, I'm going to let you search out experts or books by experts on nutrition and physical health so you can get the most up-to-date information on how to get or stay physically fit. I encourage and trust you to do what you need to do. I do have a few questions, though, to help get you thinking about what you need to do.

❦ How are you doing nutrition wise? What we eat has a lot to do with how depressed we are. Are you eating in a healthy way? Are you drinking enough water? Grade yourself on the scale (0 = My habits are endangering my life; 10 = I'm doing everything I should be doing to stay healthy).

0   1   2   3   4   5   6   7   8   9   10

❀ If your answer is not "10," what do you need to do to get healthier in the area of nutrition?

❦ How about exercise? Are you keeping in shape? Grade yourself on the scale (0 = My habits are endangering my life; 10 = I'm doing everything I should be doing to stay healthy).

0   1   2   3   4   5   6   7   8   9   10

❀ If your answer wasn't "10," what do you need to do to be healthier in the area of exercise?

❦ How about rest and relaxation? Are you getting enough sleep? Grade yourself on the scale (0 = My habits are endangering my life; 10 = I'm doing everything I should be doing to stay healthy).

0   1   2   3   4   5   6   7   8   9   10

❀ Again, if you didn't score "10," what do you need to do to be healthier in the area of rest and relaxation?

Moving On

Those are two of my four suggestions on conquering depression. Only two more to go. We're moving right along, aren't we! The next two ideas are a bit more complex but extremely important. What are they? *Change your self-talk* and *Get outside yourself.*

Let's launch into the third one right away.

Deceived

When I was in a state of depression some years ago, I discovered how deceptive it can be. Your emotions can fool you into questioning or not knowing what's real or not real. For instance, I began having fainting spells. I was in the beauty shop one day, and—clunk—down I went. After this happened a few times, my doctors said to go to the hospital for tests. What we found out is that I really wasn't fainting at all. When people faint, they aren't aware of anything going on around them. They're "out cold." But when I was "out," I knew all that was going on around me.

I guess the fainting was my body's way to get my attention. It was something that would cause people to look after me or see about me, and maybe that's what I was also craving. And it made me pay more attention to what was happening with me. Yes, I know this may sound strange, but depression can cause some strange symptoms. The bottom line was that depression was the primary culprit.

Never Normal Again?

My daughter Vikki wants to share what she learned through her lovely daughter about the importance of the way we think when it comes to depression.

> When Marsaille was born, her tongue was still attached to the bottom of her mouth, her pinky finger was twisted, and the doctors said she had a hole in her heart.

> I thought that my baby would never be normal (as we usually define normal). At first it was hard to not become depressed about the condition of my darling daughter. But I realized I had a choice, so I chose to ask God to guard my heart and keep my mind sane. I needed help in praying, so I asked my mother and my sister to pray with me. I began to concentrate on what was right with Marsaille instead of what was "wrong," and I became stronger and stronger in my faith.

> Many people prayed for Marsaille and me, and I believed the prophecy given about her—that she would be great in the kingdom of heaven.

> We went through the surgery to "unleash" her tongue. The hole in her heart closed without any surgery. As for her finger—well, I think it's cute; it makes her special. Marsaille is beautiful, smart, warm, happy, loving, and awesome. I thank God for her every day. I believe in God!

> I discovered that sometimes depression is a choice. We can think ourselves into or out of depression. My choice was to live in the present, knowing that God held my future and the future of my child in His loving hands.

> God is able to do exceeding abundantly according to His will for us. He will help us handle the things that might ordinarily depress us. Keep looking up to the hills from where our help comes. God has given us the ability to overcome situational depression by trusting in Him for all things.

Did you catch this statement: We can think ourselves into or out of depression?

Chondra Pierce, who graciously wrote the foreword to this book, is a Christian comedienne who went through a debilitating 18-month battle with depression. Courageously she wrote about her experiences in a book entitled *Depression: Journey Back to Laughter.* In a CBN interview about the book, Chondra said:

> You would be surprised at how your mind can trick your body, and your very being, that life is sad and over and done and you'll never get out of this. That is such a lie that depression uses to keep you in bondage. The truth of the matter is that's not so. *Depression is treatable.* It is something you can be *completely victorious* over. God sometimes chooses to heal miraculously, and many times He chooses for us to learn the discipline of taking care of these earthly vessels that we are trapped in until Jesus comes.

She also shared, "You've got to talk to your depression like it's a third person. You just have to say, 'You know what? Right now you are lying to me. You are telling me I can't get out of this bed and I will never amount to anything, and that's a lie.'"

So often in our experiences of depression, we reach a point of inner paralysis and stagnation. We may lose touch with the people and many of the realities around us. We may lose our sense of confidence and our resilience in the daily challenges of life. We can't seem to get our focus off ourselves. And yet all this extra attention we give ourselves doesn't lead to healthy and wholesome and wise discoveries about who we really are as God's created and redeemed children. Instead, our self-focus mostly sees only negative things.

Because depression can be so deceptive in how it affects our thoughts and what we're telling ourselves, it's vitally important that we identify the skills in how to encourage ourselves.

Our Own Captive Audience

Do you talk to yourself? Do you ask yourself questions? Do you answer those questions? Do you sometimes interrupt yourself before you get an answer? If you do, you are in good company. Most of us do these things. I do it all the time. I drive along in the car, just talking away to myself. Yes, people look over at me with strange looks. When they do, I have a response down pat. I look down and put my hand on the radio and pretend I'm singing while I turn up the volume.

Yes, people talk to themselves. *Sane* people talk to themselves. Absolutely. But when we talk to ourselves, we need to watch what we're saying. You see, when we talk to ourselves, we *invoke our consciousness*. And in our conscious awareness, we truly hear what we say. Our subconscious hears it—and believes it! Then our creative self-conscious gets busy working it out.

I'm told that if you keep telling yourself something negative (and untrue) about yourself for just 21 days, it will come to pass. You'll change, actually becoming what you've been telling yourself. Your *behavior* will reflect your thoughts. Isn't that scary? I've heard people say some pretty negative things…and I've even said them a time or two myself. Can you relate to any of these?

- I can't do anything right.
- I just can't get anywhere on time.
- I'm so sick and tired of being sick and tired.
- I'm so clumsy.
- I don't know what to do.
- I'm so dumb.
- I'm just slow.

And maybe you've been around people who keep repeating this one:

- Life is hard…and then you die.

People really talk to themselves this way. And it puts them on a downward spiral that won't stop. Why? Because the words we say can depress us.

Or they can lift us up! Yep, that's the flip side. If you keep reminding yourself of the things that are wonderful and true about you, and you affirm yourself like that for 21 days, your behavior will start to reflect those truths.

Affirmations

I love affirmations. An affirmation is a positive statement spoken in the first-person singular, present tense, as if it's already true. (And it's something that *will* be true! That's what keeps it from being a lie.) If you repeat affirmations to yourself, you're on the way to having positive self-esteem, which is biblical. After all you were created on purpose by the God of the universe! Self-esteem essentially reflects the way you talk to yourself. Here are some great affirmations to incorporate into your life—and I hope you will!

- I like myself.
- Things work out for me.
- I am healthy.
- I am blessed.
- I cherish the gift of life.
- My future is secure.
- In my heart and soul I am forever young.
- I have all the money I need to do everything God wants me to do.

(Okay, did I hear laughter on that last one?)

If you keep telling yourself wonderful truths, you allow God to move in your life more easily. And if you work and do your part, He will certainly do His.

So change the way you talk to yourself. And the right way of talking to yourself starts with the right *thoughts* in your mind.

Yes, it's true that our emotions and our wills (our hearts and souls) must also be involved, along with our intellects. But it's the engagement of the truth *with our minds* that occupies the critical place at the *start* of this process. And to get the right thoughts inside our heads—to get the *truth* engraved there—God has given us His Word in strong, clear language that we can grasp with His help.

A New Mind

In Ephesians 4:21-24, we discover something unprecedented that can take place in our way of thinking:

> [You] were taught in him, as the truth is in Jesus, to put off your old self, which belongs to your former manner of life and is corrupt through deceitful desires, and to be renewed in the spirit of your minds, and to put on the new self, created after the likeness of God in true righteousness and holiness.

✿ According to these verses, what are you told to do "in the spirit of your mind"?

Here's something fresh and different that's made possible for us—something *revolutionary* and *transformational!* This command isn't fully helpful for us if we don't know *how* to live it out, but knowing the command is there is a great start. And since God gave us this command, then *it must be possible to obey it* (with the Lord's help).

✿ And after you do what you're told to in the "spirit of your mind," what do you do next?

Romans 12:2 says,

> Do not be conformed to this world, but be transformed
> by the renewal of your mind, that by testing you may
> discern what is the will of God, what is good and accept-
> able and perfect.

❀ How does this help your understanding of the Ephesians passage?

❀ How do you think this process of mental transformation can
help you in your battle against depression?

❀ How do you think you can best go about experiencing this
transformation in your thoughts and attitudes?

❀ Why is it important that you start talking to yourself in the
right way *now*?

4

Exploring Your Expectations

Expectations can be funny things, can't they? I've told you about all those complications that arose after my hysterectomy—and how all my plans and expectations for the holidays and for the next year of my life went out the window:

- Cook a family feast for Christmas? Forget it.

- Celebrate the New Year with church friends? Not happening.

- Teach a weeklong class in January for Master's International Divinity School? Class canceled.

- Lead the weekend retreat in February for my Daughters of Zion mentoring program? Sisters, you'll have to retreat without me.

- Show up in Fort Lauderdale for the next Women of Faith National Conference? You've got to be kidding.

Pajama Mama

About the only expectation I was able to fulfill was my pajama plan.

Before I had surgery, I didn't like pajamas. To be honest, they seemed way too staid and boring for me, fashionable sexpot that I am! I was more into negligees and girly stuff. But one day, long before I knew I was going to have surgery, I happened upon a rack of pajamas during a shopping trip, and they really appealed to me. And if you know me at all, you know how I like stuff on my clothes—shiny and sparkly things. Well, these pajamas had little sequins around the bottom of the pants, and the tops had little sequins plus little satin ribbons. I looked at those pajamas and thought, *They are too cute! I wouldn't mind walking around the house with these on, even if they are pajamas.* I bought seven pairs.

And then I didn't wear them. After all, they were pajamas—and I don't like pajamas. I decided maybe I would give them as gifts. But I didn't do that either.

Then several months later, when I found out I was having surgery, I thought up the pajama plan. I knew my daughters and friends would be helping me during my recovery (which I expected to be *very* brief), and I didn't want them seeing all the sexy negligees in my dresser drawer. (I didn't want to shock them. Let's face it: No daughter wants to think of her mother wearing anything that comes from Victoria's Secret, let alone anything from Fredericks of Hollywood. And my friends? Well…)

So I took out the sexy negligees and put my bling-bling pajamas in there, along with some flowing caftans and lots of cute socks. I pictured myself during my recovery time coming into the bedroom after I showered each morning and telling my friends or my daughters to help me: "Sugar, look over there in that drawer and get me those green-and-black pajamas."

Then they would look in there and find them, and they'd think, *Oh, this looks just like Mom (or Mama T)—so fun and yet so modest.*

Of all the plans I had for those many months following my surgery, my pajama plan was the only one that came to fruition. Even then, after I started wearing those new pajamas, I wore them a long, long, *long* time—way longer than I planned or wanted.

Worth a Laugh

The rest of my look-slick-while-sick plan was a total failure. For instance, I also bought some bling-bling warm-up suits to wear in the hospital after the surgery, thinking I would be a well-heeled-while-healing hostess reigning graciously over the groups of visitors who dropped by my hotel…er…hospital room.

I also sat my children down before I left for the hospital and told them, "You all are to keep my nails looking good. Don't let my polish get chipped. And keep my feet looking cute. Don't let my heels get rusty with calluses. And you're to rub me down with sweet-smelling stuff and put makeup on my face and make sure my hair looks good. Put a little perfume on me too. And keep my room clean. Do you hear me?"

I had my little makeup case packed with everything they would need to keep me suitably turned out.

But do you think after my surgery that I cared one whit about *any* of that? My girls told me they did just as I had instructed them to, but by then I didn't know—or care—whether they did it or not.

I do remember puckering my lips once when a friend came to visit, indicating to her that I needed some Carmex (my lips were so dry!). But my friend didn't know what Carmex was for, and so she opened that little can and put that stuff all over my face. She didn't know it's only for lips. She greased me up so good that when I tried to open my eyes, my eyelids pushed up a big wad of Carmex all the way to my eyebrows.

Looking back, I now laugh at all the plans I made for my doctor, my family, and my body to follow in getting through my surgical adventure in an efficient and satisfactory manner. My experience gave me new appreciation for this little quip: "If you want to make God laugh, tell Him your plans." I had so many expectations…so many that I eventually kissed goodbye.

On Your Own Horizon

When you're tempted to be downcast and despondent, here are three big clarifying questions to ask:

- What am I expecting?

- What am I confident about?

- What do I most deeply desire?

By honestly assessing yourself in these areas, you can very often see your way up into hope.

> In regard to your overall outlook on the future, are you mostly expecting it to turn out well or to turn out poorly? Circle your answer on the graph (0 = I think things are likely to turn out extremely bad; 10 = I expect things to turn out great).

0 1 2 3 4 5 6 7 8 9 10

> How much of your outlook do you think is a result of your choices, and how much is the result of outside influences you can't control?

> My own choices: _____%

> Outside influences: _____%

Even Christians who have the strongest hope and the most positive expectations for their futures struggle at times with doubts, fears, and concerns. But those struggles typically don't shake up their *core* state—their deep-rooted belief in a positive and blessed future.

> When it comes to your deepest expectations about your future, how positive are you? Circle your answer (0 = totally negative; 10 = perfectly positive).

0 1 2 3 4 5 6 7 8 9 10

Your deepest expectations about your future greatly influence your attitudes and actions *today*. Your present behavior will *always* be affected by your outlook on tomorrow. This is why God is so concerned that you have an accurate understanding of His *control* of your future and His *plans* and *promises* for your future.

❧ Today's culture tries to get us to forget about our future and to live only for the moment—for the pleasures (real or imagined) of the present. In what ways have you seen or experienced this kind of influence?

❧ What negative effects have you noticed in your life or the lives of your family and friends from this kind of cultural influence?

Your Expectations of God

When it comes to a biblical perspective, the topic of expectations is all wrapped up in what the Bible calls "hope." That's a rich and wonder-filled word! We all hope and long for various things, yet there's also a single, unified expectation that we share with every Christian sister and brother. Paul, in his letter to the Ephesians, calls it "the one hope" that we're all called to and invited to share in. Ephesians 4:1-16 says:

> I...urge you to walk in a manner worthy of the calling to which you have been called, with all humility and gentleness, with patience, bearing with one another in love, eager to maintain the unity of the Spirit in the bond of peace. There is one body and one Spirit—just as you were called to *the one hope* that belongs to your call—one Lord,

one faith, one baptism, one God and Father of all, who is over all and through all and in all. But grace was given to each one of us according to the measure of Christ's gift. Therefore it says,

"When he ascended on high he led a host of captives,
    and he gave gifts to men."

(In saying, "He ascended," what does it mean but that he had also descended into the lower parts of the earth? He who descended is the one who also ascended far above all the heavens, that he might fill all things.) And he gave the apostles, the prophets, the evangelists, the pastors and teachers, to equip the saints for the work of ministry, for building up the body of Christ, until we all attain to the unity of the faith and of the knowledge of the Son of God, to mature manhood, to the measure of the stature of the fullness of Christ, so that we may no longer be children, tossed to and fro by the waves and carried about by every wind of doctrine, by human cunning, by craftiness in deceitful schemes. Rather, speaking the truth in love, we are to grow up in every way into him who is the head, into Christ, from whom the whole body, joined and held together by every joint with which it is equipped, when each part is working properly, makes the body grow so that it builds itself up in love.

🔅 As you reflect on this passage, what do you think Paul means by "the one hope"?

❀ What encouragement does this give you?

❀ Hope springs from God's grace. What do you know already about God's grace that gives you the most reason for hope about your future?

❀ When it comes down to it, *why* can you expect God to do good for you in the future? What is there about God's heart and character that makes this a necessity and a reality you can count on?

Romans 12 gives you three little words that can bring you so much satisfaction. What are they? "Rejoice in *hope*." And if you ask God, He will enable you to obey this simple command.

Rooted in the Facts

Our biblical hope is rooted in our appreciation for two great facts: 1) the resurrection of Jesus Christ as a historical event, and 2) His promise to return. The apostle Peter tells us that because Jesus rose from the dead, we've been "born again to a *living hope*" (1 Peter 1:3). Not a faint hope, or a slim hope, or a limp and lifeless hope. No, a hope that is alive! And this is sparked by what happened to Jesus in the grave. Have you thought about that lately?

❀ While Jesus was lying there, how dead was He?

✾ And when He came out, how alive was He?

✾ How does He prove today that He's still alive?

✾ And how will He prove He's alive in the future?

✾ What is your connection to the historical fact that Jesus rose from the dead?

Jesus not only rose from the dead, but He also ascended into heaven. And there He is keeping something for you—something that's intimately connected with your "living hope":

> Blessed be the God and Father of our Lord Jesus Christ! According to his great mercy, he has caused us to be born again to a living hope through the resurrection of Jesus Christ from the dead, to an inheritance that is imperishable,

undefiled, and unfading, kept in heaven for you, who by
God's power are being guarded through faith for a salvation ready to be revealed in the last time (1 Peter 1:3-6).

❧ What is being kept in heaven for you?

When Everything Changed

Sometimes we fail to appreciate how radically the resurrection of
Christ changed everything. We forget the revolutionary transformation it caused in humanity's understanding of eternity.

In the Old Testament, God's people sometimes had prophetic flashes
of insight into their future eternal life with God, but they also had
moments when this understanding was very limited. The full picture
didn't emerge until "Christ Jesus...abolished death and brought life
and immortality to light through the gospel" (2 Timothy 1:10).

David was one of the Old Testament saints who had his moments
of restricted sight. He wrote Psalm 39 in a time of personal suffering
and pain. He knew he was being disciplined by God, and he hated how
he felt. Because his death seemed just around the corner, he wanted
God to lighten up and leave him alone for a while. His last words in
this psalm are expressed to God:

> Look away from me, that I may smile again,
> before I depart and am no more!

That's not exactly an expression of hope, is it? David felt he had
nothing to wait for. He just wanted some time to smile again. Have
you ever felt like that? But even with such a heavy outlook, David had
written these lines in verse 7:

> And now, O Lord, for what do I wait?
> My hope is in you.

"Lord...my hope is in you." David was honest enough and wise enough to realize that only God could restore a more positive and realistic outlook in him. In fact, that desire on David's part is the reason this psalm was written. Psalm 39:10-11 says:

> Remove your stroke from me;
>   I am spent by the hostility of your hand.
> When you discipline a man
>   with rebukes for sin,
> you consume like a moth what is dear to him;
>   surely all mankind is a mere breath!

❈ Can you relate to how David regarded God's discipline of him? Have you ever thought God was being hostile toward you? That He was taking away what was dear to you? How did that feel?

❈ Perhaps there have been moments when you could relate to the bleak perspective on the afterlife David expressed in verse 13: "Look away from me, that I may smile again, before I depart and am no more!" Have you felt that your death would truly be the end of your story? What made you feel that way?

The Heart of Hope

To truly *hope* for the return of Jesus is also to *love* His return. Isn't that the truth? Paul, when he is nearing the end of a life marked by trials and dangers, tells Timothy, "There is laid up for me the crown of righteousness, which the Lord, the righteous judge, will award to me on that Day, and not only to me but also to *all* who have loved his appearing" (2 Timothy 4:8). How about you? Is *your* heart set upon the return of your loving Savior and Lord? If it is, then you know that there is a wonderful inheritance waiting for you! (Yes, this verse is for *you*—notice that word *all* near the end of it.)

❧ What is awaiting you in heaven, according to Paul's words to Timothy?

❧ How would having a heart that looks forward regularly to the return of Christ help you persevere, to endure in the face of sufferings and trials?

❧ What distinguishes this from "escapism"?

I'm encouraging you to make *hope* a *habit!* Here's a great idea! Memorize 1 Peter 1:3-6 and 2 Timothy 4:8 so you can remind yourself of the hope you have in Christ when difficulties arise.

Our Eternal View

There's something the apostle John was especially looking forward to *seeing* in eternity—something that all God's children will witness:

> ²Beloved, we are God's children now, and what we will be has not yet appeared; but we know that when he appears we shall be like him, because we shall see him as he is. ³And everyone who thus hopes in him purifies himself as he is pure (1 John 3:2-3).

❈ Why do you think this will be a wonderful sight for Christians?

❈ Did you notice what verse 3 said? The very process of looking forward in hope to this wonderful sight brings a *cleansing* to our lives right now. Take a moment to express to your heavenly Father your willingness to trust Him for this cleansing.

❈ How can the expectation of spending eternity with Jesus help you and motivate you to live a better life today and for the rest of your earthly life?

Forever Young

Only those who have a vibrant hope for the future are *truly young*. We've got an entire eternity stretching out before us, so we're just getting started in the adventures of the Christian life! It's right to feel young and stay young in our hearts. But those who have low expectations for the future will surely grow old before their time.

I don't have to ask which one of those scenarios you want to be true for you. *Forever young* or *prematurely old?* No question about the best choice there. And it's our degree of *hope* that makes the real difference. In fact, the stronger our hope, the younger we'll ultimately become. Are you ready for that?

❀ When you think of being timelessly and continuously young in your spirit, what does that mean to you? What does it look like?

❀ To help you visualize this, reflect on 2 Corinthians 4:16: "So we do not lose heart. Though our outer nature is wasting away, our inner nature is being renewed day by day." How is this revealed in your life?

Hoping for Righteousness

The words we find in Galatians 5:5 are a brief yet comprehensive statement of an experience which is the exact opposite of depression: "Through the Spirit, by faith, we ourselves eagerly wait for the hope of righteousness." This "hope of righteousness" is our expectation of rightness—of right standing with God through Jesus Christ. This hope means we can say with assurance, "I *know* I'll be all right."

> ✿ Can you see how Galatians 5:5 offers treasure for your mind and heart to dwell on for encouragement? What reaches your heart the most in the midst of your depression?

> ✿ What are the hardest words for you to accept?

> ✿ Ask your loving heavenly Father to strengthen your experience of the Holy Spirit and your faith. Write out your prayer.

A Helmet of Hope

In His loving protection for us, our heavenly Father encourages us "to put on...for a helmet the hope of salvation" (1 Thessalonians 5:8). The time is coming when we'll live with our Lord in perfect freedom and fulfillment. And if we look ahead and anticipate its coming, we can use that knowledge as a helmet to guard our minds against depression and guide our thoughts in healthy, positive ways. All this is possible because of the simple fact of what God has destined for us: "God has not destined us for wrath, but to obtain salvation through our Lord Jesus Christ, who died for us so that whether we are awake or asleep we might live with him" (1 Thessalonians 5:9-10).

⚙ What do these two verses mean to you? How can they help you today?

The Voice of Hope

Hope and prayer always go together. In fact, *prayer is the voice of hope.* When there's hopelessness, prayer dries up and blows away. Jesus invites us to pray to God, "Your kingdom come, your will be done" (Matthew 6:10).

⚙ What attitude about the future does Jesus want you to have? Based on this, do you need to change anything in your life?

Real hope is *huge!* As we discussed earlier, to have biblical hope is to possess "*living* hope." This means we can be excited and thrilled about the future even though it's unknown. We can be eager for each day knowing that our knowledge of what's happening today may be limited, but someday we'll see the fullness of God's plan and love and provision. As it is now, we can rejoice in the greatness and vastness of God that is exhibited all around us.

True freedom comes from hope—a freedom that is fresh and growing and alive. Our true and healthy hope based in our relationship with Jesus Christ can overcome uncertainty if we keep our focus on Him. When we do that, we relax our grip, we loosen our clinging fingers that have been tightly wrapped around our earthly relationships, plans, expectations, and possessions. And as we ease our grip, we can freely open our hands to receive what our loving Lord has for us.

In Whose Hands?

Did you know that just because someone *seems* bubbly and energetic and spontaneous, that doesn't mean that he or she necessarily has a clear and positive picture of the future? Sometimes people live for the moment, giving little thought to the future. They may feel they've basically "arrived," having reached "success" in whatever ways they define it. They are content in their worlds, not wanting to grow in any way, especially spiritually. They suppress or ignore the reality that life is a *process* filled with opportunities to learn and mature and develop strength spiritually, emotionally, and physically. We have so much to learn! And though it may sound easier and safer to focus on getting the most fun out of now, growing brings new capacities for experiencing contentment, fulfillment, and satisfaction.

Now, I'm not opposed to having fun and enjoying the present moment—but that shouldn't happen by ignoring the future and the eternal perspective God wants us to keep. Unfortunately, people who ignore or neglect those things tend to not pray very much. Their concentration is on building security in the pleasantness and comfort of the moment instead of actively looking toward the future and what God has for them next. They tend to want to control their lives instead of giving them to God.

❈ When it really comes down to it, how much of your need for security are *you* trying to build into your life right now? How much of your security and life are you willing to place in God's hands by depending on His promises?

❄ As you look back on this chapter, what are the most valuable affirmations of truth you need to incorporate into your daily life? How will you do this?

5

Your Perception of Reality

Perhaps the worst thing about depression is that it's *a denial of reality*. We're not believing the truth about ourselves, about God, and about our relationship with Him. And if we're not believing the truth, we are, in essence, believing lies. And that means we're listening to Satan because he's the father of lies, right? (See John 8:44.)

Miracle Among the Daisies

The reality restoring discovery of hope is a miracle, as the following story shared by a woman through my website illustrates.[1]

> Many years ago a miracle happened amidst the wild daisies growing along the road, where the bees frolicked each morning.
>
> The miracle occurred again at high noon on the mossy rocks surrounding the icy artesian waters of the frog pond...and again in the afternoon as I dug my toes in the sand and searched for quartz gems and shell treasures in the wavy shallows of the lake.
>
> I discovered hope.
>
> It didn't happen instantly, as is the usual expectation for just about everything these days. We're all too eager to be

rescued by everything from instant oatmeal to instant debt recovery. No, this was a deeper and subtler work…God's work…and He rarely is obvious or quick when He works in our hearts. And yet the change was *real*.

Most of the time my home was defined by the runaway anguish of two parents consumed either by anger (my father) or depression (my mother). Although I vicariously learned all too well the lessons of fear, inadequacy, doubt, and suspicion, I also grew to trust a regular place of respite: our lake cottage.

Each summer my inner turmoil—that squeamish, sickening blackness in my soul—was burned away by the brilliance of millions of diamonds on the water. Red-winged blackbirds called me beyond despair from their swaying perches atop the cattails. Cute but clumsy tadpoles in the creek proved it was possible to grow beyond waggling and acquire powerful legs—to actually *go* places!

I began to believe I shared more than a casual acquaintance with the lake. In fact, we developed a committed relationship. I embraced its many moods—from storm-tossed and boiling with white caps to glassy and silky smooth. The lake never let me down but without reservation shared each day with me—the real deal. No masks, no pretense, no false faces.

It wasn't until decades later that I began to understand what really happened during those sun-warmed days when we lived in my father's hand-built cabin along the shores of the lake. But eventually *I saw clearly*. God supernaturally intervened to heal me and prepare me for the rest of eternity. He faithfully prepared my wounded and guarded heart to *believe* in something mysterious, greater than myself, unchanging, refreshing, renewing, and hopeful.

Later I would realize how the lake experience prevented my heart from becoming permanently hardened. I might have otherwise entered my adult life emotionally crippled—mistrustful and reclusive. But Truth prevailed! During my days at the lake, the One who created it methodically instructed me. I was schooled in what it meant to have faith—to trust and believe.

Then one day when He whispered my name and said, "Come." His voice sounded just like the whisper of the waves—and I took the plunge.

❀ What reality did God open this person's eyes to?

❀ Have you had an experience similar to this? What can you remember about the experience? Why is it meaningful for you?

Sense of Belonging

Very often depression seems to be caused entirely from oppressive forces weighing down on us, yet the pressure is also felt deep within us. It seems to paralyze our souls. In these times of dark despondency, we allow ourselves to be taken over by the depression. In fact, that often *seems* unavoidable. Depression seizes possession of us. And we might lose for a time our vital awareness of the fact that *we belong to God*.

I'm sure you recall that this issue of "belongingness" is something we explored earlier. And it's well worth revisiting.

Let's look at the following Scripture passages that affirm our belongingness to God. Now, I know that if you're in the midst of battling depression, these messages from God may seem lifeless and distant right now. That's okay. I'm not asking you to feel what you don't feel right now. But ponder these verses and be objectively aware of the wonderful truths that may have gotten dulled and deflated in your mind due to the depression that clouds your perceptions.

Write down the main point that each passage is making in regard to God's relationship with His people.

> Know that the LORD, he is God!
> It is he who made us, and we are his;
> we are his people, and the sheep of his pasture
> (Psalm 100:3).

❧ What main point does this verse make regarding your relationship with God?

> You are my sheep, human sheep of my pasture, and
> I am your God, declares the Lord GOD
> (Ezekiel 34:31).

❧ What main point does this verse make regarding your relationship with God?

> You are Christ's, and Christ is God's (1 Corinthians 3:23).

❖ What main point does this verse make regarding your relationship with God?

> You are a chosen race, a royal priesthood, a holy nation, a people for his own possession, that you may proclaim the excellencies of him who called you out of darkness into his marvelous light. Once you were not a people, but now you are God's people; once you had not received mercy, but now you have received mercy (1 Peter 2:9-10).

❖ What main point does this verse make regarding your relationship with God?

There's an insistence in Scripture, even if it's not prominent in your heart at the moment, that *you belong to God*. And, amazingly, there's also a true sense that *God belongs to you!* Have you thought about that before? Isn't that the essence of what people mean when they say, "He is *my* God"? On that topic, let's look at more scriptures.

> Behold, God is my salvation;
> I will trust, and will not be afraid;
> for the LORD GOD is my strength and my song,
> and he has become my salvation
> (Isaiah 12:2).

❖ What main point does this verse make regarding your relationship with God?

Fear not, for I am with you;
be not dismayed, for I am your God;
I will strengthen you, I will help you,
I will uphold you with my righteous right hand
(Isaiah 41:10).

- What main point does this verse make regarding your relationship with God?

They desire a better country, that is, a heavenly one. Therefore God is not ashamed to be called their God, for he has prepared for them a city (Hebrews 11:16).

- What main point does this verse make regarding your relationship with God?

The one who conquers will have this heritage, and I will be his God and he will be my son (Revelation 21:7).

- What main point does this verse make regarding your relationship with God?

In this beautiful belongingness we can understand and recognize that what we truly and most deeply long for in life is the assurance that God loves us, that He has always loved us, and that His purpose toward us is *all good*. More than anything else, the *hope* that God's Word teaches us to hold on to is grounded in the certainty in our souls that God loves us.

> ✵ How often do you say aloud, *"God loves me"?* This is a true statement about your relationship with God. Why not purpose to say this three times a day for the next month. Does this seem odd? It means that God is no longer a stranger. Will you do this?

> ✵ Come back to this book and note the results. God's truth will work in your heart with positive results!

In the certainty that God loves us, we can also realize that He forgives those whom no one else would forgive; He loves those whom no one else would love; He accepts those whom no one else would accept. That's why God can (and does!) give us hope in circumstances where we might otherwise feel *there is no hope*.

Reality As a Created Being

Sometimes our tendency to depression is rooted in our forgetting that God *made* us. He created us. What does that mean? What does that fact mean personally to you?

❄ Think back on the last 24 hours. In all that you experienced, what evidence was there that you were created by God? That you were not an "accident" or an evolved biological phenomenon, but *you are someone designed and fashioned and formed supernaturally by the Supreme Being.*

When you seriously consider that *God created you,* what do you think His perspective is on that? And what does He want you to understand about it? Take to heart what He tells you in Genesis 1:27: "God created man in his own image, in the image of God he created him; male and female he created them."

❄ From this verse, what do you think He wants you to recognize most about the way He created you?

Now think for a moment about what Genesis 1:27 is saying. You are created in God's image. Let's take that to a more personal level.

❄ How are you most like God?

❄ How are you most different from God?

❀ What do you think are the appropriate attitudes and perspectives for a created being to maintain in her relationship with her Creator?

When you better grasp the truth about who you are as a created being, you can more easily take in the reality of who you are as a *new creation* in Jesus Christ and what He did for you on the cross. Let's explore our "new creation" status.

> If anyone is in Christ, he is a new creation. The old has passed away; behold, the new has come (2 Corinthians 5:17).

❀ What important principle(s) did you discover in the 2 Corinthians verse?

> We are his workmanship, created in Christ Jesus for good works, which God prepared beforehand, that we should walk in them (Ephesians 2:10).

❀ What important principle(s) did you discover in the Ephesians verse?

Do not lie to one another, seeing that you have put off
the old self with its practices and have put on the new self,
which is being renewed in knowledge after the image of
its creator (Colossians 3:9-10).

☙ What important principle(s) did you discover in the Colossians verses?

The Danger

We must not forget there's a real danger in depression. Spiritually
speaking, depression is not a minor ailment. No, it's a major concern.
Depression tries to disconnect us from God. We lose sight of who He
is and who we are in Him. Depression is extremely dangerous, especially if we've reached the point of despair. But God has given us many
assurances about our true identity in Him to counter any negative
thoughts and beliefs. Take a moment to look the following verses over.
Think about what each one says about *who you really are*.

For he is our God, and we are the people of his pasture,
and the sheep of his hand (Psalm 95:7).

☙ How can this verse help you avoid falling into despair?

He was wounded for our transgressions; he was crushed for
our iniquities; upon him was the chastisement that brought
us peace, and with his stripes we are healed (Isaiah 53:5).

⚙ How can this verse help you avoid falling into despair?

You were straying like sheep, but have now returned to the Shepherd and Overseer of your souls (1 Peter 2:25).

⚙ How can this verse help you avoid falling into despair?

See what kind of love the Father has given to us, that we should be called children of God; and so we are. The reason why the world does not know us is that it did not know him (1 John 3:1).

⚙ How can this verse help you avoid falling into despair?

And we all, with unveiled face, beholding the glory of the Lord, are being transformed into the same image from one degree of glory to another. For this comes from the Lord who is the Spirit (2 Corinthians 3:18).

⚙ And how can this verse help you avoid falling into despair?

One passage that is rich in revealing who we are in Christ is Ephesians 2:4-10:

> But God, being rich in mercy, because of the great love with which he loved us, even when we were dead in our trespasses, made us alive together with Christ—by grace you have been saved—and raised us up with him and seated us with him in the heavenly places in Christ Jesus, so that in the coming ages he might show the immeasurable riches of his grace in kindness toward us in Christ Jesus. For by grace you have been saved through faith. And this is not your own doing; it is the gift of God, not a result of works, so that no one may boast. For we are his workmanship, created in Christ Jesus for good works, which God prepared beforehand, that we should walk in them.

❈ Which statements about your true identity in this passage can motivate you the most? Which one touched your heart the most…and why?

Circles of Reality

Think about these two things:

- Who am I really right now?

- Who does God want me to be (and made me to be)?

❈ Now, if you were to draw a circle to represent each of these two things—would the circles overlap? If yes, how much? Go ahead and draw the two circles so you get a visual of where you're at regarding knowing the truth about your identity in Christ.

◉ In reality—in God's eyes (which is, ultimately, the *only real* reality)—wouldn't the two circles *perfectly* overlap? Even right now, at this point in time? Or do you think that is only "theoretically speaking"?

In our everyday experiences we see how often our sins and weaknesses make their appearances. But do those things represent *who we really are?* Check out Romans 6:5-11:

> If we have been united with him in a death like his, we shall certainly be united with him in a resurrection like his. We know that our old self was crucified with him in order that the body of sin might be brought to nothing, so that we would no longer be enslaved to sin. For one who has died has been set free from sin. Now if we have died with Christ, we believe that we will also live with him. We know that Christ being raised from the dead will never die again; death no longer has dominion over him. For the death he died he died to sin, once for all, but the life he lives he lives to God. So you also must consider yourselves dead to sin and alive to God in Christ Jesus.

◉ According to these verses, how are you to view your present and the future? Do you need to make any changes?

It's Personal

✿ "Hope is personal." Think about that statement a moment. Do you agree? Why or why not?

The book of Job is one of the oldest parts of the Bible (maybe the oldest). Job's life story includes great suffering...and also great hope. Read Job 19:25-27, and notice how often he uses the word "my":

> For I know that my Redeemer lives,
> and at the last he will stand upon the earth.
> And after my skin has been thus destroyed,
> yet in my flesh I shall see God,
> whom I shall see for myself,
> and my eyes shall behold, and not another.
> My heart faints within me!

✿ How would you summarize Job's hope? What truths does this passage offer you even though thousands of years have passed since Job lived?

The Anchor We Need

In the Scriptures we read about "the hope set before us" (Hebrews 6:18), but so often we lose sight of it...or lose our passion for it. God knows that, for He's well aware of our frailties, our forgetfulness, our humanness. So He did something about it. He gives us *strong encouragement* to hold fast to the hope we have in Jesus. How did God make this possible? He gave us, through Abraham, a vital promise, *and* He confirmed it by an oath:

> For when God made a promise to Abraham, since he had no one greater by whom to swear, he swore by himself, saying, *"Surely I will bless you and multiply you."* And thus Abraham, having patiently waited, obtained the promise. For people swear by something greater than themselves, and in all their disputes an oath is final for confirmation. So when God desired to show more convincingly to the *heirs of the promise* the unchangeable character of his purpose, he guaranteed it with an oath (Hebrews 6:13-18).

❧ That promise is just a few words long (but such words!). Write down God's promise to Abraham…and to you.

Most certainly, most emphatically, *God will bless you and multiply you.* As believers in Christ, we are all heirs to the promise God made to Abraham. It belongs to us just as much as it did to Abraham! That's why we can be so sure God is with us regardless of how we feel.

❧ How has God *already* blessed and multiplied you?

❧ What ways do you want God to bless and multiply you today?

❋ And in the future?

❋ How are you making this known to God? What have you specifically prayed for?

Because of this promise of blessing—guaranteed by God's oath—and because of the strong encouragement it gives us, the hope we cling to is described as "a sure and steadfast anchor of the soul" (Hebrews 6:19).

❋ What does an anchor do for a ship?

❋ Why does your soul have need for an "anchor"?

Isn't that great news? God has given you an anchor for your hope! When the storms of life come, you can grab hold of this anchor and rest in the safe harbor of God's promise to bless you. But there's more!

The wonderful hope described in Hebrews 6 *goes* someplace. It takes us somewhere:

> We have this as a sure and steadfast anchor of the soul, a hope that enters into the inner place behind the curtain, where Jesus has gone as a forerunner on our behalf, having become a high priest forever after the order of Melchizedek (verses 19 and 20).

The curtain in the Jewish temple separated the "Holy of holies" from the rest of the building. Behind the curtain was the ark of the covenant. The Holy of holies was where God resided.

❈ What do you think "the inner place behind the curtain" means?

❈ Who has already gone there?

The *Bible Knowledge Commentary on the New Testament* adds a helpful note to the anchor imagery. The anchor we cling to has been

> carried to the safest point of all—the inner sanctuary behind the curtain—by Jesus, who went before us...[Staying with the harbor imagery, this] recalls the role of sailors who leave their ship in a smaller craft in order to carry the anchor forward to a place where it can be firmly lodged. So too the Lord Jesus, by His entrance into the heavenly sanctuary where He functions as a High Priest forever,

has given to a Christian's hope an anchorage from which it cannot be shaken loose.[2]

❈ What is Jesus doing on your behalf?

The book of Hebrews is rich with meaning and Old Testament imagery. I hope you'll read and study the entire book soon to explore the wealth of wisdom it offers. Meanwhile, you can rest in the wonderful confidence that Jesus is your high priest forever and works on your behalf (Hebrews 6:20).

Source of Hope

Romans 15:4 is such an assuring reminder for us because it indicates a trustworthy source for our hope—all by God's design:

> For whatever was written in former days was written for our instruction, that through endurance and through the encouragement of the Scriptures we might have hope.

What does this verse indicate about God's attitude toward you and me? That God's Word is *a trustworthy lens on reality* for us—as well as our source of hope.

❈ How can you experience God's Word more fully? What steps will you take to get into this treasured resource more often and more deeply?

❀ Why do you think God has given so many promises in His Word?

❀ What does this tell you about the attitude of His heart toward you?

❀ How do you think He wants these promises to assist you? What role(s) does He want them to fill in your life?

❀ As you look back on this chapter, what are the most valuable affirmations of truth you need to incorporate into your daily life? How will you do this?

Responding to Hardship

When things don't work out the way we plan...

When we're handed loss while hoping for a blessing...

When our rewarding work suddenly collapses into rubble...

When someone or something we love is taken from us...

When any bad thing happens, the potential for the light in our lives going out is great. We often become lost, not understanding why calamity has swept through our lives and dumped us in a dark place devoid of hope. We compare what we expected and longed for with what actually happened, and our hearts break as we cry out and question God. *Why, Lord? Why me? Why now? Why this?*

The truth is that we may never know this side of eternity why God sometimes allows us to stumble forlornly through the valley of the shadow of death. But if we reach out to God and pull ourselves closer to Him, He will reach out to comfort and encourage us. Then we can look for advantages in each adversity.

Advantage in Adversity?

I shared with you the troubles I went through following my hysterectomy (see introduction: "Our Journey Together"). Because of the complications, I was essentially housebound for more than six months and disabled for several months after that. On top of having to give up the events and activities I'd scheduled and worked toward—all of them entertaining, rewarding, and (I thought) essential for me—I endured pain like I'd never known before (and hope never to know again). For all I'd given up, for all I'd lost, I grieved and cried and complained to God.

But when all that gnashing of teeth and wearing of pajamas was done, when I settled into a quiet routine of being home all day, all week, all month, I found an advantage in my adversity. I was growing closer—ever closer—to my Savior, my Lord, my God. When I realized I was going to be home all day with nothing "important" happening, I found I didn't have to rush through my morning prayers. I didn't have to read one chapter of my Bible and then shove it into my computer bag before rushing off to the airport. I could read the entire book of Esther or the entire Gospel of Matthew—plus commentary notes! I could sing through several psalms, opening my heart to God's wisdom and joy. And after that I could meditate on what I'd read, and I could pray at length about the concerns of my heart. I let God fill every hour of my day and every inch of my heart—and it was *good!*

Since then I've spent time considering the discomfort I endured from the surgery and complications—the overwhelming pain, the time in the intensive care unit, the blood transfusions, and the hallucinations caused by medications. I've wondered if I could or would ever be strong enough and courageous enough to *choose* to go through that terrible ordeal if it would spare someone I love from enduring it. And then I thought of how trivial my experience seems compared to the prolonged agony Jesus *chose* to endure on my behalf—the humiliating trial, the brutal beatings, the splintery weight of the cross on His bleeding shoulders as He hauled it toward Calvary, the crown of thorns piercing His brow, the spikes pounded into His hands and feet, the agony of death by crucifixion.

When I think of it, I wonder, *Why, Lord? Why me? How could You go through so much to save a wretch like me?* And the answer rolls over me like warm, soothing breeze on a cold day: *Love. Because I love you.*

I learned so much during those long months of heartache. While the world swirled on without me, I grieved for the independence I'd lost…but I also eventually reveled in the enlightenment I gained during my recovery. And I can tell you in all truth that the terrible situation was one of the best things that ever happened to me.

That's *not* saying I would eagerly go through it again. But I see now how much I learned about my Savior and what He did for me (and you!) during that time. I cherish the deeper relationship I have with Him that came about because of being "forced" through adversity to draw closer to Him.

Alcoholism and Unemployment

Here's another testimony from someone who learned from adversity. This woman shared her story on my website, www.ThelmaWells.com.

> My story is one of faith and walking through trials to have the life the Lord intended. Though I was in the depths of alcoholism, unemployment, and physical abuse, I always knew God had a better way for me.
>
> I was brought up in the Lord but drifted away in my twenties. At the time, nothing in my life seemed to go right. I left a high-paying career due to mental depression and crippling anxiety. I married a man who abused me physically, mentally, and emotionally for many years. There were times I had to move back in with my parents even though I was well into my forties. In ten years I had eight jobs and drifted from place to place.
>
> Finally I called out to God in desperation. Now I am sober, I've divorced my abusive husband, and I'm back to working and living on my own. I recently served on a mission trip to Guatemala.
>
> The Lord has restored my life and given me true Christian peace and joy this time!

In a Burning House

And here's another testimony shared on my website:

Back in February our house burned down around me. I was the only one at home, and when I woke up the house was totally engulfed in flames except for our bedroom.

I opened the bedroom door, and all that was there was a wall of flames. I had nowhere to go!

I started screaming for my husband, but I never heard anything except the roar of the fire. I tried to knock out either of the windows in our bedroom, but they wouldn't budge.

I was screaming and crying. I begged God not to let me die like this. Then it was if He just reached down and wrapped His arms around me. I had a peace that was unbelievable. I was able to think clearly. I took a comforter off the bed, wrapped up in it, and ran through the fire. I managed to get out of the house alive. *Thank You, Lord!*

I was burned badly, but I am alive. I owe every breath I breathe to our precious Lord. I know that I'm still alive because God isn't done with me yet.

It's really strange in a way—my husband and I were having some marital problems, and it seems that after I was well into recovery, and with the help and direction of God, our marriage is better than ever.

❧ What about you, friend? What can you learn from the adversity you're facing? What are you telling yourself when hardships crash into your life?

Incurable Wound

I've been watching the prophet Jeremiah for a number of years through his words in the books of Jeremiah and Lamentations. I've been mesmerized by his incredible 40-year ministry, and how his prophecies were so linked to the fate of his nation.

Jeremiah reminds the children of Israel that error and disobedience in their lives and their failure to take God seriously was dangerous and would destroy them. But the people didn't take Jeremiah seriously. They paid no attention to what he said. In fact, they might have thought he was crazy. Like most humans, the people enjoyed doing their own things and following their own interests.

Jeremiah told them God was going to send judgment and punishment—that they were going into 70 years of captivity, exile, and slavery if they didn't stop their wicked rebellious ways.

But they still didn't listen.

Not surprisingly, this was depressing to Jeremiah. He cried with a sorrowing heart over the future and plight of the people and the fact that they did not listen to him. Speaking to God, he said, "I sat alone, because your hand was upon me, for you had filled me with indignation" (Jeremiah 15:17). In his depressed state he asked, "Why is my pain unceasing, my wound incurable, refusing to be healed?" (verse 18).

Jeremiah thought the Lord had abandoned him. But God reminded Jeremiah that He hadn't abandoned or forgotten him. He was with him all the time.

And isn't that what we all want to know in times of despair? When we're depressed, don't we want to hear a word from our Lord? Jeremiah certainly did. And God continued to speak to him and stay with him. But God also promised that Jeremiah's prophecies wouldn't find receptive ears and hearts among the people:

> I will make you to this people a fortified wall of bronze; they will fight against you, but they shall not prevail over you, for I am with you to save you and deliver you, declares the LORD. I will deliver you out of the hand of the wicked, and redeem you from the grasp of the ruthless (Jeremiah 15:20-21).

When people don't understand us, when family and friends shun us, when the world is calling us ignorant and stupid because we follow and serve Jesus, we must come to grips with the fact that not everyone will understand or choose to live for Jesus. We aren't responsible for this. We can't *make* someone listen or come to the Lord. We don't need to—and we shouldn't!—take the emotional rap or become depressed. We only have to do what Jeremiah finally did. He found his hope and strength and purpose in God.

Times of Trouble

In the time of a terrible drought, as the prophet Jeremiah prayed for help, he said to God, "O you hope of Israel, its savior in time of trouble..." (Jeremiah 14:8). This can also be a pattern for *your* prayers as well as mine. We can start our petitions with "O Jesus, my hope, my Savior in time of trouble..." Jeremiah shows us that biblical hope includes an *expectation of deliverance* from troubling situations.

> ✿ Are you in a "time of trouble"? If so, what expectations of deliverance do you have from God?

Was your answer "none at all"? If so, please don't despair. Don't give up. Instead, let's think through this together and keep moving forward through the darkness until a light begins to shine and a gentle rain falls on the thirsty ground of your soul. Let's turn again to Jeremiah. He prayed again, calling God "the hope of Israel" and expressing these words of hope:

> Heal me, O LORD, and I shall be healed;
> save me, and I shall be saved,
> for you are my praise (Jeremiah 17:14).

Yes, the Lord God is our hope for *healing* as well as *deliverance*.

❀ Do you talk to God with as much confidence as Jeremiah does? If you were going to pray like Jeremiah, what would you say to God?

Something New Every Morning

The book of Lamentations, which is believed by many to be written by Jeremiah, was obviously written from the darkest depths of affliction. The third chapter is the heart of the book, and it is especially helpful for us as we assess our responses to the afflictions that come our way. Let's look at the first 18 verses.

> I am the man who has seen affliction
>   under the rod of his wrath;
> he has driven and brought me
>   into darkness without any light;
> surely against me he turns his hand
>   again and again the whole day long.
>
> He has made my flesh and my skin waste away;
>   he has broken my bones;
> he has besieged and enveloped me
>   with bitterness and tribulation;
> he has made me dwell in darkness
>   like the dead of long ago.
>
> He has walled me about so that I cannot escape;
>   he has made my chains heavy;
> though I call and cry for help,
>   he shuts out my prayer;
> he has blocked my ways with blocks of stones;
>   he has made my paths crooked.

He is a bear lying in wait for me,
    a lion in hiding;
he turned aside my steps and tore me to pieces;
    he has made me desolate;
he bent his bow and set me
    as a target for his arrow.

He drove into my kidneys
    the arrows of his quiver;
I have become the laughingstock of all peoples,
    the object of their taunts all day long.
He has filled me with bitterness;
    he has sated me with wormwood.

He has made my teeth grind on gravel,
    and made me cower in ashes;
my soul is bereft of peace;
    I have forgotten what happiness is;
    so I say, "My endurance has perished;
    so has my hope from the LORD."

❁ What stands out to you about this man's condition—physically, emotionally, and spiritually?

❁ How would you summarize this man's view of God?

❀ Notice especially the two things this man says he lost in the last verse. What are they, and how are they related?

Even with this man's profound disappointment with God, and his loss of hope, he still turns to the Lord in prayer:

> ¹⁹Remember my affliction and my wanderings,
>   the wormwood and the gall!...
> ²⁰My soul continually remembers it
>   and is bowed down within me.
> ²¹But this I call to mind,
>   and therefore I have hope:
> ²²The steadfast love of the LORD never ceases;
>   his mercies never come to an end;
> ²³they are new every morning;
>   great is your faithfulness.
> ²⁴"The LORD is my portion," says my soul,
>   "therefore I will hope in him."

❀ What specific mental action does he take in verses 21-23, and what change does this bring about in his attitude?

Verse 24 is a beautiful expression of *faith* and *commitment*. The *Bible Exposition Commentary* explains:

> If the Lord is "our portion" (Psalm 73:26; 142:5), then we are strengthened by that which cannot be used up or destroyed. God is our eternal source of strength, hope, and blessing (Psalm 46:1). Our circumstances change, and

so do our feelings about them, but God is always good, loving, merciful, and kind, and He never changes. "Jesus Christ is the same yesterday, today, and forever" (Hebrews 13:8 NKJV). To build life on that which is always changing is to invite constant unrest and disappointment, but to build on the changeless and the eternal is to have peace and confidence.[1]

⚑ According to Lamentations 3:24, what does the writer of Lamentations believe? What does he commit to?

⚑ Applying this verse to your life, what do you think it means for your soul that "the LORD" is your "portion"?

⚑ Does this truth give you a glimpse of hope? If it does, why not stop right now and write it down, and then tell God how grateful you are for this and why.

The Risk of Hope

Quickly read Romans 5:1-5.

> ¹Therefore, since we have been justified by faith, we have peace with God through our Lord Jesus Christ. ²Through him we have also obtained access by faith into this grace in which we stand, and we rejoice in hope of the glory of God. ³More than that, we rejoice in our sufferings, knowing that suffering produces endurance, ⁴and endurance produces character, and character produces hope, ⁵and hope does not put us to shame, because God's love has been poured into our hearts through the Holy Spirit who has been given to us.

Surely one of the most *risky* verses God included in His Word is verse 5. *Hope doesn't put us to shame.* As the NKJV translates it, "Hope does not disappoint." Now, this may get intense, but please stay with me. How many times have you and I had our earthly hopes dashed? How many times has disappointment dragged us down into dejection, embarrassment, and shame? And all because our expectations weren't met. The hope God wants to cultivate inside us isn't situational or fluid with ups and downs. God realizes our sufferings on a more realistic level.

> ❄ Did you notice that our hope is directed toward God's glory? "We rejoice in hope of the glory of God" (verse 2). What is it about God's glory that *you* look forward to experiencing or observing?

Ours is also a hope that arises from the development of our life-seasoned, trial-toughened character (and that takes time!): "We rejoice in our sufferings, knowing that suffering produces endurance, and endurance produces character, and character produces hope" (verses 3 and 4). Everybody experiences suffering, and lots of people respond to it with bitterness, complaining, or emotional paralysis. But a blessed few choose to respond to their suffering with character-producing endurance...that eventually will bear the fruit of a richer, stronger, deeper hope.

⌘ In your opinion, what makes positive endurance possible?

⌘ What makes this kind of endurance so valuable for character growth? How does that process work?

⌘ What current issues or situations in your life do you need to respond to with endurance?

⌘ Since hope is the *product* of character, does that mean experiencing depression, which is lack of hope, is a sign of a lack of character? Can the flaws in our character sometimes be the source of our depression?

If that is true, then it's so important to yield to God's plans and purposes for our lives *as He shapes our character* through suffering. Right?

❋ How is God shaping your character through suffering right now? What seeds of hope is He planting in your soul because of your suffering?

Our hope is *guaranteed!* How? Because "God's love has been poured into our hearts through the Holy Spirit" (Romans 5:5). Our gracious God is teaching us that our hope is fundamentally tied to *our experience of His love in our hearts.* Has God's love been poured into your heart? Do you *know* that for sure?

❋ If you're certain God's love has been poured into your heart, talk to God (in writing) about what that's been like.

❋ And if your answer is *no,* you haven't experienced God's outpouring of love, I encourage you to spend some time meditating on Romans 5:6-11:

> For while we were still weak, at the right time Christ died for the ungodly. For one will scarcely die for a righteous person—though perhaps for a good person one would dare even to die—but God shows his love for us in that while we were still sinners, Christ died for us. Since, therefore, we have now been justified by his blood, much more shall

we be saved by him from the wrath of God. For if while we were enemies we were reconciled to God by the death of his Son, much more, now that we are reconciled, shall we be saved by his life. More than that, we also rejoice in God through our Lord Jesus Christ, through whom we have now received reconciliation.

❀ What does God say He has done for you personally to open your heart to receive His outpouring of love? Express this in your own words and share what it can mean for your life.

7

A Troubled Man's Cry

Are you willing to listen in for a moment to the cries and groans of a good man as he's overwhelmed by trouble? Things could hardly have been worse for David than they were at the time he wrote Psalm 38. Physically he was wounded and sick—and he knew it was a result of his sin and folly. Morally, he knew he was guilty. Don't turn aside from this troubled man. Receive his words and learn from him as he shares his hurts with us so honestly:

PSALM 38
¹O LORD, rebuke me not in your anger,
   nor discipline me in your wrath!
²For your arrows have sunk into me,
   and your hand has come down on me.
³There is no soundness in my flesh
   because of your indignation;
there is no health in my bones
   because of my sin.
⁴For my iniquities have gone over my head;
   like a heavy burden, they are too heavy for me.
⁵My wounds stink and fester
   because of my foolishness,

⁶I am utterly bowed down and prostrate;
    all the day I go about mourning.
⁷For my sides are filled with burning,
    and there is no soundness in my flesh.
⁸I am feeble and crushed;
    I groan because of the tumult of my heart.

⁹O Lord, all my longing is before you;
    my sighing is not hidden from you.
¹⁰My heart throbs; my strength fails me,
    and the light of my eyes—it also has gone from me.
¹¹My friends and companions stand aloof from my plague,
    and my nearest kin stand far off.
¹²Those who seek my life lay their snares;
    those who seek my hurt speak of ruin
    and meditate treachery all day long.
¹³But I am like a deaf man; I do not hear,
    like a mute man who does not open his mouth.
¹⁴I have become like a man who does not hear,
    and in whose mouth are no rebukes.
¹⁵But for you, O Lord, do I wait;
    it is you, O Lord my God, who will answer.
¹⁶For I said, "Only let them not rejoice over me,
    who boast against me when my foot slips!"
¹⁷For I am ready to fall,
    and my pain is ever before me.
¹⁸I confess my iniquity;
    I am sorry for my sin.

¹⁹But my foes are vigorous, they are mighty,
    and many are those who hate me wrongfully.
²⁰Those who render me evil for good accuse me
    because I follow after good.
²¹ Do not forsake me, O Lord!
    O my God, be not far from me!
²²Make haste to help me,
    O Lord, my salvation!

❃ What words and phrases does David use to describe his physical hurt (verses 3-10)?

❃ What are the words and phrases that acknowledge his wrong-doing?

❃ How are people treating David in his low condition (verses 11-12,19-20)?

❃ Did you notice how David responds in his prayer? According to verse 15, what did he want God to know?

❃ What do you think was involved for David in "waiting" on God this way?

✿ While he "waited," what did David do about his sin (verse 18)?

Read verses 21 and 22 and imagine what was going on in David's heart. Because you're human and have had many trials here on earth, I'm sure you've felt the same way David felt. You've probably known much the same condition in your own heart.

✿ How are David's words in verses 21-22 right and appropriate for when you feel this way?

When Sin Is in the Picture

It's sad but true that sometimes depression is the direct result of our sinful actions. After all, sin is dark and dirty business, and it damages everything in its path. "But even now there is hope" (Ezra 10:2). Isn't that a wonderful statement? It's especially refreshing because the speaker was answering for the widespread and grievous sins of the people. Speaking for them, Shecaniah says, "We have broken faith with our God." And that was true. They had been faithless toward God, and they broke His commandment to not marry and be involved with the people of the land they occupied. Yet still they found hope for forgiveness and restoration as they pursued the difficult path of repentance and submission to God through Ezra's prayerful leadership.

Even when we've stumbled into sin and broken faith with our loving God—*even then there is hope!* There is hope because God has shown us the way out of our shameful defeat. Meditate on 1 John 1:9:

> If we confess our sins, [God] is faithful and just to forgive
> us our sins and to cleanse us from all unrighteousness.

Isn't this a great message of hope? And God's Word provides plenty of other assurances that God loves us and cares for us and will restore us…even though we have sinned and fall short of His glory.

> Come now, let us reason together, says the LORD:
> though your sins are like scarlet,
> they shall be as white as snow;
> though they are red like crimson,
> they shall become like wool (Isaiah 1:18).

- What are the most important words to believe and hold on to in the previous verse from Isaiah if you're sunk in a depression brought on by sin?

> Let the wicked forsake his way,
> and the unrighteous man his thoughts;
> let him return to the LORD, that he may have compassion on him,
> and to our God, for he will abundantly pardon
> (Isaiah 55:7).

- What are the most important words to believe and hold on to in this verse?

> I tell you, there is joy before the angels of God over one
> sinner who repents (Luke 15:10).

❀ What are the most important words to believe and hold on to
in this verse from Luke?

> Repent therefore, and turn again, that your sins may be
> blotted out, that times of refreshing may come from the
> presence of the Lord, and that he may send the Christ
> appointed for you, Jesus, whom heaven must receive until
> the time for restoring all the things about which God
> spoke by the mouth of his holy prophets long ago (Acts
> 3:19-21).

❀ What are the most important words to believe and hold on to
in this passage from Acts?

Every moment in this life we have the "freedom" to sin. But very
soon, in the eternal presence of our holy God, we'll no longer be bothered by sin. Won't that be a glorious relief!

Finding Security

Are you needing security? David needed it desperately in a time
of affliction that he describes as a "pit of destruction" and a "miry
bog." Read Psalm 40:1-3 to discover how David's need for security
was met:

> I waited patiently for the LORD;
>   he inclined to me and heard my cry.

He drew me up from the pit of destruction,
　　out of the miry bog,
and set my feet upon a rock,
　　making my steps secure.
He put a new song in my mouth,
　　a song of praise to our God.
Many will see and fear,
　　and put their trust in the LORD.

✿ What was David doing?

✿ What did God do in response?

Because of this experience, David had hope and confidence in God when he faced ordeals. Check out verses 11-12 in this psalm:

As for you, O LORD, you will not restrain
　　your mercy from me;
your steadfast love and your faithfulness will
　　ever preserve me!
For evils have encompassed me
　　beyond number;
my iniquities have overtaken me,
　　and I cannot see;
they are more than the hairs of my head;
　　my heart fails me.

✿ How would you describe David's situation?

❀ How would you describe his hope? What was he anticipating?

Are you anticipating the same thing? If not, why not make David's attitude and words your own? I encourage you to memorize the 17 verses in Psalm 40. It's a wonderful encouragement when troubles assail you.

Hopelessness

Life can get hard—and the man in the Bible named Job had it harder than most. At one point at least, the afflictions that battered him left him feeling hopeless. And it's completely understandable. Here's what he says about his existence:

> Has not man a hard service on earth,
> and are not his days like the days of a hired hand?
> Like a slave who longs for the shadow,
> and like a hired hand who looks for his wages,
> so I am allotted months of emptiness,
> and nights of misery are apportioned to me.
> When I lie down I say, "When shall I arise?"
> But the night is long,
> and I am full of tossing till the dawn.
> My flesh is clothed with worms and dirt;
> my skin hardens, then breaks out afresh.
> My days are swifter than a weaver's shuttle
> and come to their end without hope.
> Remember that my life is a breath;
> my eye will never again see good (Job 7:1-7).

Can you relate to Job's feeling of misery and hopelessness? Once wealthy and a well-respected husband and father, Job's life took a very hard turn. His livestock was killed or stolen, his children were killed in a catastrophe, his servants were murdered, and he lost all his wealth. But Job worshiped the Lord even during his grief. Then Job was afflicted with a disease that caused painful sores all over his body. His wife said, "Do you still hold fast your integrity? Curse God and die." Job's friends wondered if Job had committed grievous sins that brought about punishment from God. Job complained and questioned the Lord about why His blessing was removed.

But Job didn't stay in this condition of hopelessness. In his mind and soul, Job kept wrestling over his condition. He eventually found a ray of hope. He felt sure he was about to die, but he found hope in the midst of despair. We get a glimpse of this in Job 13:15 where he says of God, "Though he slay me, I will hope in him." Job complained bitterly, and the Lord God came and rebuked him. Then Job humbled his heart and confessed to his audacity, "I have uttered what I did not understand, things too wonderful for me, which I did not know...I had heard of you by the hearing of the ear, but now my eye sees you; therefore I despise myself, and repent in dust and ashes."

And the Lord in His mercy accepted Job's prayer...and blessed him by restoring his fortunes and enabling him to have a new family.

You have joy and hope in the Lord God who created the heavens and the earth and all that is. Even in the midst of sorrow, praise His majesty and loving care for His creation...and for you.

What You and God Can Do

When we experience depression, we sometimes sink to such a low point that we believe there's nothing we can do to make life better. And if that were true, it would be depressing. But that's not true! That mindset loses sight of reality. *Feeling* powerless and incapable doesn't mean we *are* powerless. And realizing that we have the ability to change things isn't enough either. We have to *exercise* that ability. To move forward, we've got to believe in Jesus *and* act on that belief.

And we can and will move forward when we realize afresh how God has given us promises about the abilities that *He* makes possible within every one of His children:

And God is able to make all grace abound to you, so that having all sufficiency in all things at all times, you may abound in every good work (2 Corinthians 9:8).

✿ What's the personal reality for *you* in this promise from 2 Corinthians? What does it have to do with what *you* are able to do?

Now to him who is able to strengthen you... (Romans 16:25).

Now to him who is able to do far more abundantly than all that we ask or think, according to the power at work within us... (Ephesians 3:20).

Now to him who is able to keep you from stumbling and to present you blameless before the presence of his glory with great joy... (Jude 24).

✿ Drawing on these three verses, what kind of life path is God spreading out before you? In what ways have you seen each of these truths played out in your life?

Now may the God of peace himself sanctify you completely, and may your whole spirit and soul and body be kept blameless at the coming of our Lord Jesus Christ (1 Thessalonians 5:23).

I'm praying this blessing from Paul for you. Cling to its truths and draw strength and comfort from knowing God loves you, cares for you, and provides for you.

Skilled in Lowness

Paul once stated honestly, "I know how to be brought low" (Philippians 4:12). He was skilled in lowness. From the context of his letter to the Philippians (as well as his other letters), we know Paul faced severe hardships and the utmost in depressing circumstances. *He learned how to respond to these.* He didn't just "suck it up," grit his teeth, or use "positive thinking." He didn't deny the reality of his troubles and try thinking happy thoughts instead. No, Paul said he learned "the secret" of finding contentment "in whatever situation." That secret? "I can do all things *through him who strengthens me*" (verse 13).

Yes, there are times when you and I are "brought low." This is an inescapable part of the journey God is taking us on. So our goal is to be able to say with assurance, "I know how to handle that." *With God, I know I can make it through this.* No, it isn't easy, but there is a way to do it: by depending on the only One who can effectively strengthen us for such trials.

❀ According to Philippians 4:13, what is the secret of finding contentment when we've been "brought low"?

❀ Describe what *you* have learned so far about your depression. Note any changes you've made and the results. For instance, are you more confident in Christ as the solution? Has your self-talk become more encouraging?

8

Looking Outward

May I burst your bubble?

The world doesn't revolve around you.

I know you thought it did. I used to think the same thing about me. But I discovered it doesn't. The final item on my list for coping with depression involves *reaching out to others.* One of the best ways to deal with depression is to do something for somebody without expecting anything in return.

When I was depressed, one of the "prescriptions" I got from my doctor was to get involved in something larger than myself. My doctor was very insightful. I tried it—and it worked. I encourage you to find a way to help. Search for a volunteer organization whose cause you support and lend a helping hand. Many schools have programs for mentoring children who have difficulty reading. Humane Societies and pet shelters can always use people. If the work seems disagreeable, you can spend time petting and playing with the animals—something they need for their health and to help them socialize with people. Going to nursing homes to visit with the elderly who don't have families in the area is another great opportunity…and you might learn a lot about the "good old days." Do *something.* That's the key. You help yourself when you help others. There are a lot of people out there who need you.

The Drive for Connection

Let me tell you a family story that demonstrates our human need for others.

> One of my daughters had a job that required a great deal of travel. Her little girl spent many nights away from her beloved mommy. Because of their attachment to each other, my daughter would have to wait until the baby went to sleep and slip away if she was going to work out of town.
>
> When the baby would awake and ask for her mother, the answer she would get was, "Mommy's gone to work. She'll be back to get you really soon." This went on for three years, and in those three years we observed a progressively unhealthy clinging to her mother. The child wanted to be with her mom constantly, every minute of every day and night.
>
> As the little girl grew to understand more of what her mother was doing, she became afraid to go to sleep if she and her mother were not at home. When someone other than her mother would pick her up from daycare, she would pitch a fit because she realized her mother wouldn't be home for a few days. Even when the child was cared for by responsible family members who loved her dearly, she would become irritable, anxious, angry, stubborn, and sullen. She began saying, "Why me? Why is Mom leaving me?"
>
> When her mother was at home, the little girl was dancing and prancing, lively and vivacious as she busily spent her time drawing, painting, singing, and playing. She was secure knowing her mom was right there.

This situation was a reminder to me that one of the basic human drives of mankind is to *be connected to someone*. We love affiliation, affection, and association when it is comfortable and calming. This is the same attention that the little girl was craving from someone she had bonded with—her mother.

And in a sense, it's something that none of us ever grows out of.

Getting Outside Yourself

> God is not so unjust as to overlook your work and the love that you showed for his sake in serving the saints, as you still do. And we desire each one of you to show the same earnestness to have *the full assurance of hope* until the end (Hebrews 6:10-11).

Did you notice that "the full assurance of hope" is something we can possess and take firm hold of? Being truly serious about possessing this hope is marked by a certain kind of lifestyle—a lifestyle of *loving to be of service to others.*

❧ Perhaps you're already working very hard, with genuine love, in serving your Christian brothers and sisters. If you are, this passage says that *someone is noticing.* Who is it?

❧ What does this mean to you? How does it make you feel?

Peter's Experience with Hope and Love

Someone who doesn't believe in the Lord won't experience the same degree of triumphant hope for the future that a Christian does. And yet the flip side is also true. In some ways believers can experience despair more intensely than nonbelievers. This happens when a believer is persuaded (in error) that he or she can't please God. This person lives in fear of God's wrath and condemnation.

Do you remember when the apostle Peter was standing in the courtyard outside the place where Jesus was being held after being arrested? The time when Peter denied Christ three times, just as Jesus had told him he would? Let's look at what happened.

> Now Peter was sitting outside in the courtyard. And a servant girl came up to him and said, "You also were with Jesus the Galilean." But he denied it before them all, saying, "I do not know what you mean." And when he went out to the entrance, another servant girl saw him, and she said to the bystanders, "This man was with Jesus of Nazareth." And again he denied it with an oath: "I do not know the man." After a little while the bystanders came up and said to Peter, "Certainly you too are one of them, for your accent betrays you." Then he began to invoke a curse on himself and to swear, "I do not know the man." And immediately the rooster crowed. And Peter remembered the saying of Jesus, "Before the rooster crows, you will deny me three times." And he went out and wept bitterly (Matthew 26:69-75).

❃ From this passage, what do you suppose Peter was thinking? Based on his actions, what conclusions can you draw about what he expected to happen to Jesus? What predicament was Peter expecting to be in?

Peter heard Jesus foretell His resurrection (as well as His death). In those hours that Peter spent in the courtyard, his confidence in Jesus was shaken. His faith was wavering. If Peter had truly lost his faith in Jesus and his love for Jesus, he likely would have walked out of the courtyard with relief that his denial of knowing Jesus had saved him from punishment. But that's not what happened. Peter's bitter tears indicate his *heart* condition—that he still loved Jesus.

🌼 How do you think Peter would have answered the question, "How does God feel about you right now?"

🌼 Now imagine that Peter had entered that courtyard with the rock-solid assurance and expectation that Jesus was going to be killed but rise from the dead. In that case, how do you think he would have answered the people who accused him of being associated with Jesus?

Now we're going forward in time to when Jesus was resurrected and visiting with the disciples by the Sea of Galilee. Look at the conversation Jesus and Peter had (John 21:15-21):

> When they had finished breakfast, Jesus said to Simon Peter, "Simon, son of John, do you love me more than these?" He said to him, "Yes, Lord; you know that I love you." He said to him, "Feed my lambs." He said to him a second time, "Simon, son of John, do you love me?" He said to him, "Yes, Lord; you know that I love you." He said to him, "Tend my sheep." He said to him the third time, "Simon, son of John, do you love me?" Peter was grieved because he said to him the third time, "Do you love me?" and he said to him, "Lord, you know everything; you know that I love you." Jesus said to him, "Feed my sheep. Truly, truly, I say

to you, when you were young, you used to dress yourself and walk wherever you wanted, but when you are old, you will stretch out your hands, and another will dress you and carry you where you do not want to go." (This he said to show by what kind of death he was to glorify God.) And after saying this he said to him, "Follow me."

Peter turned and saw the disciple whom Jesus loved following them, the one who had been reclining at table close to him and had said, "Lord, who is it that is going to betray you?" When Peter saw him, he said to Jesus, "Lord, what about this man?" Jesus said to him, "If it is my will that he remain until I come, what is that to you? You follow me!" So the saying spread abroad among the brothers that this disciple was not to die; yet Jesus did not say to him that he was not to die, but, "If it is my will that he remain until I come, what is that to you?"

Jesus brought Peter out of his despair. He focused His disciple's attention on their love relationship and asked him to serve people in His name. And yet He also cautioned Peter that the future won't always be rosy: "When you are old, you will stretch out your hands, and another will dress you and carry you where you do not want to go."

❀ For your own healthy hope, how does the Lord want *you* to focus on your love relationship with Him?

❀ What realistic understanding might He want you to have about the not-so-fun side of your future?

When we let disappointment lead to depression and despair, we often deny our Lord and Savior by failing to see His presence and purpose in our lives. Yet even then, He is waiting for us to return to Him so He can forgive and restore us.

✦ Do you hear Him asking you to follow Him? Why is this…or would this be…so important?

In depression, we experience a sad kind of resignation that leads to inactivity and a lack of courage to step forward into the "great things"— the challenges and undertakings God brings our way. Through faith in Jesus, we can accept His call and step out of ourselves to fulfill what He asks us to do.

✦ Where are you when it comes to being ready for the tasks God has for you? Using the scale, circle the number that best represents where you are (0 = I can't even begin to take on anything new…and I don't even want to hear about it, and 10 = I'm ready and eager for any assignment from God. Bring it on!).

0   1   2   3   4   5   6   7   8   9   10

The Fear of Responsibility

Sometimes we don't even *want* to be in good emotional and spiritual health because we're afraid of the obligations and responsibilities that might come by being active in our faith in Jesus. We'd rather be "sick" (at least a little) so we can avoid demands and have excuses for avoiding work or what we perceive is work. (Even fun activities can entail some work.)

❀ What do you think God expects from you regarding your faith and service? How do you feel about this?

Let's get some guidance from the Scriptures on understanding God's call. In the first chapter of 2 Corinthians, Paul shares the affliction he, along with Timothy, experienced in Asia. He admits about this time of hardship, "We were so utterly burdened beyond our strength that we despaired of life itself. Indeed, we felt that we had received the sentence of death" (2 Corinthians 1:8-9). But they persevered, and Paul affirms, "But that was to make us rely not on ourselves but on God who raises the dead. He delivered us from such a deadly peril, and he will deliver us. On him we have set our hope that he will deliver us again" (2 Corinthians 1:9-10).

Even though answering God's call on his life was often difficult and hazardous to his health, Paul was guided by God, in love and faith, to continue to serve and reach out to believers and nonbelievers with the gospel.

❀ What does Paul say he did to move from despair to hope?

❀ How can you apply this to your life? And what will it look like?

The Big Picture

If you've accepted Jesus as your Lord and Savior, you are God's daughter...and He has plans for you.

> We are his workmanship, created in Christ Jesus for good works, which God prepared beforehand, that we should walk in them (Ephesians 2:10).

> You were called to freedom, brothers. Only do not use your freedom as an opportunity for the flesh, but through love serve one another (Galatians 5:13).

> His divine power has granted to us all things that pertain to life and godliness, through the knowledge of him who called us to his own glory and excellence...Make every effort to supplement your faith with virtue, and virtue with knowledge, and knowledge with self-control, and self-control with steadfastness, and steadfastness with godliness, and godliness with brotherly affection, and brotherly affection with love. For if these qualities are yours and are increasing, they keep you from being ineffective or unfruitful in the knowledge of our Lord Jesus Christ (2 Peter 1:3,5-8).

> And let the peace of Christ rule in your hearts, to which indeed you were called in one body. And be thankful (Colossians 3:15).

❊ In a "big picture" sense, what has God called you to? What did He create and redeem you for?

❋ What do you think God might have for you in the future? (If you're not sure, what traits and skills do you have that God might call on you to use as one of His children?)

❋ Through writing, let God know about your willingness to accept further challenges and assignments as He moves you forward into stronger emotional and spiritual health.

You're Being Watched

In 1 Peter 3:15, the apostle Peter reminds us to honor Christ as Lord in our hearts and always be ready to give a good and respectful answer to someone who asks us to give a reason for our faith. When we're stuck in depression, looking like we're living without hope, what message does this send to the people around us?

Does this sound like an impossible task? To be hopeful all the time… so that the people around you will be inspired to ask about Christ? Because God tells you in His Word to always be ready, He will give you the strength and ability to do so. I'm not saying you should fake it and pretend that everything is peachy when it's not. That's not being honest. So what can you do? Seek God every day, praying about the depression. Actively read His Word and follow His guidelines. Even in the midst of hard times, sad times, and frustrating times, you have the joy of the Lord inside you. If people can see you relying on God even when life isn't going smoothly, that sends a powerful message about God's loving care. If they can clearly see that you're pulling out of depression even though you're got every earthly reason to stay there, that might get their attention. If they wonder about it, they might ask you about it…and you'll have an opportunity to share the gospel!

> ❈ Have you thought about the people around you who might be watching how you're coping with this difficult time in your life? Are they seeing Christ in you? If not, how can you show the hope you have in Christ during this time?

> ❈ What can you do to be ready to share God's love when people ask about your hope in the Lord?

Staying Outward Focused

All of us are tempted at times to draw back from appropriate responsibilities and God-given opportunities and challenges. This desire becomes especially strong when we face unexpected hardships and setbacks and discouragements that can drive us into despondency, depression, and despair. How can we stop this downward cycle? The solution is *not* to simply fill our time with busyness. However, we often do that as a defense mechanism against facing squarely the real issues of our depression.

The *real* solution is to cooperate with God as we strive for (and pray for!) the courage and confidence to…

- *accept* that God has designed us and called us to true greatness of soul and true greatness of service to His people and to humanity (John 13:34; 20:21).

- *expect* that God will continue training us—and *never stop* (by His grace)—for His assignments as we live out the greatness we were created for and redeemed for by the blood of Jesus Christ (Titus 2:11-14).

- *experience* the thrill of expectation and eager longing for the day coming soon when we will be in the eternal presence of God. What unimaginable fulfillment and joy that will be (Psalm 16:11)!

❧ If you truly believe these things, pour out a prayer about it to your heavenly Father, and record in writing some of the phrases you used.

By God's design, these inward realities don't just happen. He wants us to cultivate them in our minds and resist the pressures of the world around us—a world that is intent on blurring or refuting these realities (by the devil's influence) in the heart and soul of every child of God. In 1 Peter 5:8-9 we're urgently reminded to stay alert to the devil's dangerous prowling, especially in light of the suffering that so many Christians experience worldwide:

> Be sober-minded; be watchful. Your adversary the devil prowls around like a roaring lion, seeking someone to devour. Resist him, firm in your faith, knowing that the same kinds of suffering are being experienced by your brotherhood throughout the world. And after you have suffered a little while, the God of all grace, who has called you to his eternal glory in Christ, will himself restore, confirm, strengthen, and establish you (1 Peter 5:8-11).

❧ According to this passage, what attitude are you to have as you resist the devil?

❀ According to this passage, what will God do for you when your earthly suffering comes to an end?

❀ "God of all grace…will himself restore, confirm, strengthen, and establish you." What do these promise words mean to you personally? What hope do they give you?

❀ Why is it ultimately prideful on our part if we refuse to accept and embrace the promises God gives for our future?

❀ How do you think God wants you to be more involved in reaching out to others in this season of your life?

9

Looking Up

The very best way I know to get outside yourself is to *look up to God,* the Author and the Finisher of your faith. God cares about you. He understands your feelings…your mood…your depression. He knows where they came from, and He knows what to do with them. But you need to change them. So give them to Him every day. He's standing by waiting to take them from you. Tell Him, *"All to You, Jesus, I surrender."*

God is the only person who's going to be with you every second of every minute of every hour of every day of every week of every year of every decade of your life. If you're in a battle with depression, let me say once more that *you're not crazy.* God knows you're not crazy. And He also has the perfect antidote for your depression. Nothing escapes Him, and He knows you far better than you know yourself. Isn't that a relief and a comfort?

From Staleness to Passion

Christians do get depressed, but it's a *temporary* state. God allows us to experience it as a means to attaining something better. Our hope and contentment are based on seeing our past and present difficulties as gifts from God to prepare us and enable us to do more for Him by sharing Christ, finding delight in God and what He ordains. I'd like to share a friend's brief story about looking up and going from staleness to passion.

> I've been a Christian since I was four. That's right, four! Oh, I didn't know all the theological intricacies that come along with our Christian faith, but I knew I did bad things, and I knew a price needed to be paid because of those things. I also believed that Jesus had paid that price for me, and I wanted that!
>
> But decades later, as an adult, I found that my faith had grown stale—without life and without a passion for Christ. Then, about six years ago, my wife of 16 years left me. I never dreamed that would happen, and regardless of who is to blame (there's enough to go around), it was the catalyst for my reawakening.
>
> Looking back, it was the "most horrible but best thing" that has ever happened to me. Did God make this happen to bring me back to Him? Oh, I'm not going down that path. But one thing I do know: He allowed it to happen for His glory and His glory alone.
>
> Today I'm 46, and I pray for my ex-wife. Not that she will recognize her horrible mistakes and the wake of suffering that was caused, but that Christ will awaken her to His glorious peace, and that she will truly find His rest—that she can die to herself so Christ can live through her. That is true rest indeed.

The Humility of Hope

Did you know it takes *humility* to have hope? That's right. When we look to the future and we're confident that God's promises will come true, that's not being arrogant or presumptuous on our part. Rather, in that process we humble ourselves by admitting that we don't have it all together *right now*—that we're still missing something significant in our lives in the present moment, and we're anticipating that God will someday fill that vacuum and void we feel. Humbleness is a sense of lowness—and we can be brought low either through circumstances that press down upon us or by our own deliberate choice.

We might feel low because a sense of depression is trying to rule in our hearts—but *down* is actually a wonderful starting place for us to experience God's reality in a fresh, upward way. The following verses reveal something about these ups and downs. Below each one, note what truth you found in it.

> The LORD upholds all who are falling and raises up all who are bowed down (Psalm 145:14).

Truth:

> The LORD lifts up those who are bowed down (Psalm 146:8).

Truth:

> The LORD lifts up the humble; he casts the wicked to the ground (Psalm 147:6).

Truth:

> Humble yourselves before the Lord, and he will exalt you (James 4:10).

Truth:

There's something very pleasing to God when we're so desperate that we cry out for His mercy. We realize a truth about ourselves that so many people never understand. And in true humility, we *expect* God's grace and mercy based solely on His mercy because we know more than ever how undeserving we are. Our eyes are on Jesus. We *expect* His grace and mercy because we know our holy God is "the Father of mercies and God of all comfort" (2 Corinthians 1:3), so rich and overflowing in grace and compassion.

The Waiting of Hope

"Waiting on the Lord." We hear that phrase a lot, don't we? But it's not just letting time go by. It means investing the time with expectation and trust while we wait for God to act on His promises. When we wait upon the Lord, the waiting we do isn't simply a shallow "positive outlook" that ignores reality. That becomes clear in Romans 8:

> [22]For we know that the whole creation has been groaning together in the pains of childbirth until now. [23]And not only the creation, but we ourselves, who have the firstfruits of the Spirit, *groan inwardly* as we wait eagerly for adoption as sons, the redemption of our bodies. [24]For in this hope we were saved. Now hope that is seen is not hope. For who hopes for what he sees? [25]But if we hope for what we do not see, we wait for it with patience.

Even while we "wait eagerly" for all that God has for us, we also "groan inwardly." This is normal for the children of God in this world.

☙ If you expressed your "inward groaning" in words at this moment, what would those words be?

☙ Verse 23 tells you to eagerly await *two things.* One focuses on your relationship with God, the other on your personal deliverance.

What are these two things, and what does each one mean for you at this moment?

❀ In verses 24-25, note that your hope *saves* you—yet it isn't something you see and possess. In your relationship with the Lord God, what do you most look forward to actually *seeing* someday for the first time?

❀ Notice in verse 25 that there's a need for *patience* as you exercise your hope. Why do you think God asks for this?

The Hope That Fills

Paul wrote a wonderful blessing to the Christians in Rome:

> May the God of hope fill you with all joy and peace in believing, so that by the power of the Holy Spirit you may abound in hope (Romans 15:13).

❀ Yes, your God is a God of hope! How has God filled you with joy and peace as you believe in Him?

❀ How can the final result Paul expresses help you in your depression?

Romans 15:13 reveals that there really is such a thing as an overflowing hope, an abounding hope, more than enough for *every* situation in your life. And it's available to you through "the power of the Holy Spirit." Although it may seem unrealistic for you to expect this kind of experience day-by-day, remember that your God is the God of the impossible! "Nothing will be impossible with God" (Luke 1:37). Abundant hope comes your way by His grace, and His grace is more than sufficient to keep you well-supplied with hope.

❀ Write a few words that capture your worship and appreciation for the God of hope and grace you serve.

In Colossians 1:27 we are pointed to the deepest source of our hope: "To them God chose to make known how great among the Gentiles are the riches of the glory of this mystery, which is Christ in you, the hope of glory." The living, dynamic presence of Jesus within us is our wellspring of hope. Jesus is hope's embodiment, and the carrier and the holder and the inspirer of our hope. This "mystery" is part of God's unfolding plan and purpose for our lives.

The Dependency of Hope

The writer of Psalm 71 needed rescuing from evildoers, and he asked for that rescue from God. When he did, he added this:

> For you, O Lord, are my hope,
> my trust, O LORD, from my youth (verse 5).

To bravely call the Lord "*my* hope" and "*my* trust" is always a step forward out of despondency. The Lord becomes your very own source. When you think about what the last line of that verse says, you might respond, "Oh, but in my youth I really wasn't trusting God that much." But look at what the psalmist goes on to say:

> Upon you I have leaned from before my birth;
> you are he who took me from my mother's womb.
> My praise is continually of you (verse 6)

This hope, this trust, this dependence on God started long before you were ever consciously aware of it! Isn't that amazing?

> ❀ As you consciously surrender and yield into this deep, deep dependence upon God, tell Him about it…and write down your conversation.

The Heights of Hope

Take a relaxed moment to look over the wonderful words of Isaiah 55:6-13:

> ⁶Seek the LORD while he may be found;
> call upon him while he is near;
> ⁷let the wicked forsake his way,
> and the unrighteous man his thoughts;
> let him return to the LORD, that he may have compassion on him,
> and to our God, for he will abundantly pardon.

⁸For my thoughts are not your thoughts,
  neither are your ways my ways, declares the LORD.
⁹For as the heavens are higher than the earth,
  so are my ways higher than your ways
  and my thoughts than your thoughts.
¹⁰For as the rain and the snow come down from heaven
  and do not return there but water the earth,
making it bring forth and sprout,
  giving seed to the sower and bread to the eater,
¹¹so shall my word be that goes out from my mouth;
  it shall not return to me empty,
but it shall accomplish that which I purpose,
  and shall succeed in the thing for which I sent it.
¹²For you shall go out in joy
  and be led forth in peace;
the mountains and the hills before you
  shall break forth into singing,
  and all the trees of the field shall clap their hands.
¹³Instead of the thorn shall come up the cypress;
  instead of the brier shall come up the myrtle;
and it shall make a name for the LORD,
  an everlasting sign that shall not be cut off.

When God speaks about His ways and thoughts being "higher" than ours (verse 9), this isn't a putdown. He isn't trying to discourage us by reminding us of our limitations and telling us to stay down low where we belong. No, He's trying to raise us up! He wants to lift our perceptions so we will recognize how full of compassion He is—even for those who are "wicked" and "unrighteous" (verse 7). He wants us all to know that He abundantly pardons.

He wants His people to realize that His purposes for us—the purposes He outlines and accomplishes through His Word—are so wonderful that it takes a beautiful, almost unbelievable picture to capture them.

❀ Gaze into that picture described in verse 12, and write down what you see.

❧ This is the hope of the children of God! Can you see yourself in this picture? *Imagine* it! As you do, what do you hear being sung by the mountains and hills while the trees clap along?

Isn't that fun and inspiring to contemplate?

The Happiness of Hope

Our hope is a "blessed hope," as Paul expresses it in his letter to Titus. It's *a happy hope!* And in the two verses leading up to that declaration, we see how God's grace is at work to *train* us in certain things:

> For the grace of God has appeared, bringing salvation for all people, training us to renounce ungodliness and worldly passions, and to live self-controlled, upright, and godly lives in the present age, waiting for our blessed hope, the appearing of the glory of our great God and Savior Jesus Christ, who gave himself for us to redeem us from all lawlessness and to purify for himself a people for his own possession who are zealous for good works (Titus 2:11-14).

❧ What evidence do you see in your life that God's grace has been busy training you in how to *wait* for Jesus and His second coming?

We don't like to wait, do we? Most of the time we just don't *feel* like waiting. But there are good reasons the Lord is having us cool our heels as we wait for everything to work out to perfection when Jesus comes back. But this passage gives us a reason for waiting.

❧ What do you think God is accomplishing in your life while you wait?

The Possession of Hope

There's a phrase in Scripture that leaves an ache in my heart: "having no hope and without God in the world" (Ephesians 2:12). *Having no hope.* Can there be a more tragic description of anyone's existence? But that is what Scripture says is true of unbelievers—and was true of all of us before we came to faith in Jesus. Thanks be to God, we are *no longer* like those who have no hope. Paul addressed this issue when writing to the Christians in Thessalonica:

> [13]We do not want you to be uninformed, brothers, about those who are asleep, that you may not grieve as others do who have no hope. [14]For since we believe that Jesus died and rose again, even so, through Jesus, God will bring with him those who have fallen asleep. [15]For this we declare to you by a word from the Lord, that we who are alive, who are left until the coming of the Lord, will not precede those who have fallen asleep. [16]For the Lord himself will descend from heaven with a cry of command, with the voice of an archangel, and with the sound of the trumpet of God. And the dead in Christ will rise first. [17]Then we who are alive, who are left, will be caught up together with them in the clouds to meet the Lord in the air, and so we will always be with the Lord. [18]Therefore encourage one another with these words (1 Thessalonians 4).

❧ What do you have to be happy and joyful about, according to verses 15-18? How does this relate personally to you?

The Superiority of Hope

The hope that you have in Jesus is called "a better hope" in Hebrews 7:19. That's because it's better than anything God's people could ever experience through the law and the Old Testament system of sacrifices. The hope we have in Jesus is better because it allows us to do something that was impossible before:

> On the one hand, a former commandment is set aside because of its weakness and uselessness (for the law made nothing perfect); but on the other hand, a better hope is introduced, through which we draw near to God (Hebrews 7:18-19).

Isn't that astounding? The God of the universe, the Creator of everything, wants you to be close to Him!

The Savoring of Hope

Each of these passages says something about the reality of the presence and personality of Jesus. They are also a part of the *reality* of your relationship with Him. Do you see and hear and feel and taste these truths in your encounters with Jesus? (Yes, all of us have plenty of room to grow in this area!)

> For each truth about Jesus, write down whether you need to take steps to more readily see this in your life. Also note how the truth encourages you.

> Again Jesus spoke to them, saying, "I am the light of the world. Whoever follows me will not walk in darkness, but will have the light of life" (John 8:12).

✿ In that day you will know that I am in my Father, and you in me, and I in you. Whoever has my commandments and keeps them, he it is who loves me. And he who loves me will be loved by my Father, and I will love him and manifest myself to him (John 14:20-21).

✿ As the Father has loved me, so have I loved you. Abide in my love. If you keep my commandments, you will abide in my love, just as I have kept my Father's commandments and abide in his love. These things I have spoken to you, that my joy may be in you, and that your joy may be full (John 15:9-11).

✿ He is the source of your life in Christ Jesus, whom God made our wisdom and our righteousness and sanctification and redemption (1 Corinthians 1:30).

✿ And he is before all things, and in him all things hold together (Colossians 1:17).

⊛ If we walk in the light, as he is in the light, we have fellowship with one another, and the blood of Jesus his Son cleanses us from all sin (1 John 1:7).

⊛ I am the Alpha and the Omega, the first and the last, the beginning and the end (Revelation 22:13).

The Nearness of Hope

Reflect for a moment on Psalm 34:18:

> The LORD is near to the brokenhearted and saves the crushed in spirit.

Think about the *responsibility* that God has taken on your behalf. Think about the *reality* that He has promised to those who are weighed down by woundedness.

❊ At this time in your life, what is the best part of this message to you from God?

Sometimes we're like one of the blind men Jesus encountered. Jesus gripped this man's hand, took him aside, spat on his eyes, and laid

His hands on him. Then the Lord asked, "Do you see anything?" And the man looked up and answered, "I see men, but they look like trees, walking." Even after concentrated effort by Jesus, there was still a need. "Then Jesus laid his hands on his eyes again; and he opened his eyes, his sight was restored, and he saw everything clearly" (Mark 8:23-25.)

And Jesus has dealt with us in an intense way as well, and we've been affected by His touch, but sometimes we still experience a lack of clarity. When we're honest with ourselves, we admit that the truths we sense with the eyes of our hearts and souls aren't always vivid and unmistakable. We need more involvement from the Lord; we need further encounters with Him.

> 🌸 Where do you sense the need for more clarity in your understanding of the Lord and what He has for you?

The Perfect Power Source

One of the primary ways you can fight depression is to bond with your heavenly Father even more. You are born of His Spirit, and He knew you before the foundation of the world. He understands your loneliness and concerns, your happiness and joy, your needs and desires, and everything on your mind—the expressed as well as the unexpressed.

When you are away from Him—when you aren't praying to Him, listening to Him speak to you, praising Him, worshiping Him, or connecting to people who love Him—that's when you become like a frightened, timid, longing, frustrated, confused, and agitated child who needs her daddy.

Some of your depression is probably a disconnect with the Spirit of God through His Son, Jesus Christ. God assures you in His Word that if you abide in Him and His Word abides in you, you can talk to Him and tell Him anything and He will bring His will to pass. Think of it like being plugged into an electric socket. You know that when you turn on an item that's plugged in, the energy is available. But when a transformer blows or the cord becomes unplugged, the energy ceases and the appliance no longer runs.

If you're depressed and you're not sure why, check to see if you've been disconnected or only loosely connected to the power source of life. Jesus is the connecting link between you and God. Jesus is sitting at the right hand of the Father's throne, making intercession for you, talking to God on your behalf! So talk to Him about anything and everything. He longs for you to confide in Him. He asks you to seek Him and call upon Him in your distress.

He loves you with a lavish love like nobody else can, and He proved it by dying on a cruel, rugged cross…and then rising from the tomb where He was buried with all authority over heaven and earth in His hands—hands that are ready, willing, and able to catch you when you are falling and help you find your equilibrium again.

When you're connected to Him, He promises to lead you in the right path and surround you with His ministering angels. When you are at the end of your resources, He promises to provide for you. When you are sick and seemingly can't get well, He promises to heal you physically, mentally, and spiritually. When your children are wayward, He says He'll redeem the children of the righteous.

Staying connected to Him allows the favor of God to move on your behalf for tuition and books for school, for transportation or a bus pass to get around, for heating when it's cold and air conditioning when it's hot, for refreshing cool water when you're thirsty and food when you're hungry, and for diapers for your babies. You and I can probably go on and on in listing what God does for you—and it's all so that you don't ever have to feel abandoned or separated from your loving heavenly Father.

Why not try to continually and regularly thank Jesus for His availability and let Him have your heart? Reality and truths aren't always readily visible to human senses. You won't always see what is around you. The Father is with you constantly. He will never leave you or forsake you. If for some reason you were abandoned by humans in the past and you're still feeling the effects of that abandonment, you can choose right this minute to connect with God through His Son Jesus and claim the benefit of being permanently connected in the ultimate love relationship.

And God has made it so easy to connect with Him! The Scriptures say that you only need to confess with your mouth that you have sinned and come short of the glory of God (everybody has), and believe in your heart that God raised Jesus from the dead, and then ask Jesus to come and live in your heart. That connects you with the true Lover of your soul…and the universe's power source.

And as you stay connected, you'll find that some of the things you enjoyed doing that weren't uplifting or healthy gradually become of no interest to you anymore. As you continue to grow and to pray, you'll find that some people you used to hang out with hold less and less interest. Your hopes, dreams, and aspirations will change to include more inspiring conversations and media. Some of the things that depressed you before will no longer be a menace. And you'll discover new areas of interest and joy.

Jesus wants you to stay connected to Him. If you do, your vision will become less and less obscured by feelings of abandonment and loneliness. Every day you'll be able to see more clearly that He is with you, always ready to offer comfort and cheer.

❂ How do you think God wants you to be more involved in reaching toward Him in this season of your life?

God Is with You!

In closing I encourage you to seek the Lord in your distress. Remember He is *always* with you. He will never leave you.

I am poured out like water,
    and all my bones are out of joint;
my heart is like wax;
    it is melted within my breast;
my strength is dried up like a potsherd,
    and my tongue sticks to my jaws;
    you lay me in the dust of death…

But you, O Lord, do not be far off!
    O you my help, come quickly to my aid!
Deliver my soul from the sword,
    my precious life from the power of the dog!
    Save me from the mouth of the lion!
You have rescued me from the horns of the wild oxen!
I will tell of your name to my brothers;
    in the midst of the congregation I will praise you:
You who fear the Lord, praise him!…
    Glorify him, and stand in awe of him…

For he has not despised or abhorred the affliction of the
    afflicted,
and he has not hidden his face from him,
but has heard, when he cried to him
(Psalm 22:14-24).

⬱

May the God of hope fill you with all
joy and peace in believing,
so that by the power of the Holy Spirit
you may abound in hope
(Romans 15:13).

Notes

Chapter 1: The Truth About Depression

1. Archibald D. Hart, PhD, "Depression," in *The Complete Book of Everyday Christianity: An A-to-Z Guide to Following Christ in Every Aspect of Life*, Robert Banks and R. Paul Stevens, eds. (Downers Grove, IL: InterVarsity Press, 1997).

2. Ibid.

3. Ibid.

4. Ibid.

5. Joe S. McIlhaney Jr., MD, and Freda McKissic Bush, M.D., *Hooked: New Science on How Casual Sex Is Affecting Our Children* (Chicago: Northfield Publishing, a div. of Moody Publishers, 2008).

6. Freda McKissic Bush, MD, is an obstetrics and gynecologist specialist and a teacher at the University of Mississippi Medical Center.

7. Psychology Information Online, http://www.psychologyinfo.com.

8. Hart, "Depression."

9. Ibid.

10. *Psychology Information Online,* www.psychologyinfo.com/depression/index.html, developed by Donald J. Franklin, PhD, copyright © 1999, 2000, 2002, 2003. All rights reserved.

Chapter 5: Your Perception of Reality

1. For more personal stories people willingly share to encourage others, visit www.thelmawells.com.

2. *Bible Knowledge Commentary/New Testament* (Sisters, OR: Cook Communications Ministries, 1983, 2000), sv. Hebrews 6:19-20.

Chapter 6: Responding to Hardship

1. Warren W. Wiersbe, *The Bible Exposition Commentary: Old Testament* (Colorado Springs: Cook Communications Ministries, 2004), sv. Lamentations 3:19-39, copyright © 2001-2004 by Warren W. Wiersbe. All rights reserved.

About the Author

THELMA WELLS' life has been a courageous journey of faith. Born to an unwed and physically disabled teenager, the name on Thelma's birth certificate read simply "Baby Girl Morris." Her mother worked as a maid in the "big house" while they lived in the servants' quarters. When Thelma stayed at her grandparents' home, her grandmother locked her in a dark, smelly, insect-infested closet all day. To ease her fear, Thelma sang every hymn and praise song she knew.

A trailblazer for black women, Thelma worked in the banking industry and was a professor at Master's International School of Divinity. Her vivacious personality and talent for storytelling attracted the attention of the Women of Faith Conference. She was soon one of their core speakers. She was named Extraordinary Woman of the Year in 2008 by the Extraordinary Women Conferences. She also received the Advanced Writers and Speakers Association's Lifetime Achievement Award in 2009.

Along with writing books, including *Don't Give In...God Wants You to Win!* Thelma is president of Woman of God Ministries. "Mama T," as she is affectionately known, helps girls and women all over the world discover Jesus and live for Him.

Thelma earned degrees at North Texas State University and Master's International School of Divinity. She was awarded an honorary Doctorate of Divinity (DD) from St. Thomas Christian College and Theological Seminary and ordained through the Association of Christian Churches in Florida.

Thelma and George, her husband of 49 years, enjoy spending time with their children, grandchildren, and great-grandchildren.

∞

For more information about Thelma and her ministry, check out
www.thelmawells.com.

God Calls You "Winner"!

Is stress, indecision, heartache, or fear zapping your energy? Popular speaker and author Thelma Wells says life doesn't have to be that way! Opening her heart and God's Word, she reveals how God taught her to stand tall to win against discouragement and oppression by putting on God's armor. You'll discover...

- what spiritual warfare is
- who you're fighting
- what you're accomplishing

Thelma's contagious energy and enthusiasm invite you to tackle life with a "can do" attitude. You'll find great ways to dress for successful spiritual battle by:

- fixing your hair
  (putting on the helmet of salvation in Jesus for safety)
- padding your heart
  (donning the breastplate of righteousness to confront evil)
- putting on your stomping shoes
  (stepping out in faith against the devil)

No human wins every fight, so Thelma encourages you to call on Jesus when you get tired. He wants you to win, and He actively participates with you to ensure victory.

It's a Brand-new Day!

Dynamic, upbeat, and always forthright, author and popular speaker Thelma "Mama T" Wells encourages you to choose joy every day…and explains how to do that even when trouble turns your world upside down.

Through biblical wisdom and powerful stories that highlight God's amazing presence, extraordinary love, and unfailing provision, you'll soon embrace Thelma's steps to welcoming each day:

- never say "never" to God
- love and spend time with your family and friends
- be liberal with praise
- talk to God about everything
- dig into God's Word

From simple strategies to in-depth approaches, Mama T shows you how to draw closer to Jesus, experience the help He offers, and put joy and contentment into your day.